Kezlah Warner

CONTROL

CURRENCY PRESS
The performing arts publisher

THE ACTORS' THEATRE

CURRENCY PLAYS

First published in 2019
by Currency Press Pty Ltd,
PO Box 2287, Strawberry Hills, NSW, 2012, Australia
enquiries@currency.com.au
www.currency.com.au

in association with Red Stitch Theatre Company

Copyright: *Control* © Keziah Warner, 2019.

COPYING FOR EDUCATIONAL PURPOSES

The Australian *Copyright Act 1968* (Act) allows a maximum of one chapter or 10% of this book, whichever is the greater, to be copied by any educational institution for its educational purposes provided that that educational institution (or the body that administers it) has given a remuneration notice to Copyright Agency (CA) under the Act.
For details of the CA licence for educational institutions contact CA, 11/66 Goulburn Street, Sydney, NSW, 2000; tel: within Australia 1800 066 844 toll free; outside Australia 61 2 9394 7600; fax: 61 2 9394 7601; email: info@copyright.com.au

COPYING FOR OTHER PURPOSES

Except as permitted under the Act, for example a fair dealing for the purposes of study, research, criticism or review, no part of this book may be reproduced, stored in a retrieval system, or transmitted in any form or by any means without prior written permission. All enquiries should be made to the publisher at the address above.

Any performance or public reading of *Control* is forbidden unless a licence has been received from the author or the author's agent. The purchase of this book in no way gives the purchaser the right to perform the play in public, whether by means of a staged production or a reading. All applications for public performance should be addressed to the author c/- Currency Press.

Typeset by Dean Nottle for Currency Press..
Cover design by Emma Bennetts.
Cover shows (from left) Samuel Rowe, Christina O'Neill, Dushan Philips and Naomi Rukavina (photo: Rob Blackburn, Black Photography).

Currency Press acknowledges the Traditional Owners of the Country on which we live and work. We pay our respects to all Aboriginal and Torres Strait Islander Elders, past and present.

 A catalogue record for this book is available from the National Library of Australia

Contents

Control

    Act One   1

    Act Two   26

    Act Three   48

Theatre Program at the end of the playtext

Control was first produced by Red Stitch Actors' Theatre at the Red Stitch Theatre, St Kilda, on 9 October 2019, with the following cast:

> ELIZABETH / NICKI / ISABELLE   Christina O'Neill
> ANDREW / ALEX   Dushan Philips
> JAKE / XAVIER   Samuel Rowe
> LAURA / CAROLINE / ESTA   Naomi Rukavina

Director, Julian Meyrick
Dramaturg, Tom Healey
Artistic Director, Ella Caldwell
Set and Costumer Design, Emily Collett
Lighting Design, Lisa Mibus
Sound and AV Design, Justin Gardam
Assistant Director, Shaun Wykes
Production Manager, Greg Clarke
Stage Manager, Alysha Watt
Assistant Stage Manager, Maxine Palmerson

This play was developed through Red Stitch's INK writing program, proudly supported by: Cybec Foundation, Lyngala Foundation, Malcolm Robertson Foundation, City of Port Phillip, Copyright Australia and our Kindred.

CHARACTERS

ACT ONE
- ANDREW, 40s, American
- ELIZABETH, 30s, not from America but lives there now
- JAKE, 20s, Australian
- LAURA, 20s, English

ACT TWO
- CAROLINE, 20s, human
- ALEX, AI
- NICKI, 30s, human
- XAVIER, 20s, human

ACT THREE
- ESTA, AI
- ISABELLE, 30s, human

CASTING

For 4 actors:
1: 40s – ANDREW, ALEX
2: 20s – JAKE, XAVIER
3: 30s – ELIZABETH, NICKI, ISABELLE
4: 20s – LAURA, CAROLINE, ESTA

For 6 actors:
1: 40s – ANDREW
2: 20s – JAKE, XAVIER
3: 30s – ELIZABETH, NICKI, ISABELLE
4: 20s – LAURA, CAROLINE
5: age not important – ALEX
6: 20s – ESTA

The cast must be diverse.

This play went to press before the end of rehearsals and may differ from the play as performed.

ACT ONE

1.

Sometime in the future.

A spaceship, hurtling towards Mars.

The ship's control centre.

JAKE *and* ELIZABETH *are fighting to control the ship.* ELIZABETH *is heavily pregnant.*

LAURA: We're not supposed to change course.
JAKE: We've got to do something.
LAURA: We're not trained to use it. It's all pre-programmed. If we start messing with / it
JAKE: There's a manual override. If we didn't need it, it wouldn't be there.
LAURA: I don't / think

The pod jerks.

JAKE: Fuck.
LAURA: It's just turbulence. We need / to

The pod jerks again.

ELIZABETH: Shit.
ANDREW: Oh god, this is it.
LAURA: What?
JAKE: This isn't it. Shut the fuck up.
ANDREW: This is why they sent us.
JAKE: I'm not just going to stand here / and
LAURA: We don't know / what we're
ELIZABETH: No, he's right. We've got to try / to
JAKE: Yes /
LAURA: Fucking hell /
JAKE: Okay, Liz, come here.

The pod jerks. It throws ELIZABETH *in the opposite direction.*

ELIZABETH: Fucking. Fuck.

JAKE: You okay?
ELIZABETH: Yeah.

    She gets to the panel.

JAKE: Look, this shows our direction so these buttons must set the course.

    ELIZABETH *points at something.*

ELIZABETH: This could be forwards and / backwards
LAURA: Can you two hear / yourselves
JAKE: We need to reverse / it so
LAURA: Stop it. Just stop it. What if you press the wrong thing and we go flying off course? We don't even know how close we are to the surface.
JAKE: We can see the surface, it's right there.
LAURA: But we don't know how fast we're going. We should let the / pod

    The pod jerks again.

ELIZABETH: Fuck /
JAKE: I'm not letting / it
ANDREW: It's the / atmosphere

    JAKE *indicates two handles.*

JAKE: Look, we need to press and turn at the same time to override it, okay?
LAURA: Andrew's right, it's the atmosphere. It means more turbulence. This is just / a bad
ANDREW: The whole ship's going to break apart.
JAKE: Fuck off, Andrew.
ELIZABETH: Okay /
LAURA: It's like on a plane, right? We're just going through the clouds.
JAKE: We're overriding it.
LAURA: Jake, don't be a fucking hero!
JAKE: What?
LAURA: Just / don't
JAKE: We haven't got time to discuss this. Liz, you take that side.
ELIZABETH: Got it.

    They position themselves.

LAURA: Jake. Please. I'm begging / you
JAKE: I'm sorry.
LAURA: Please /
JAKE: Laura. This is something I have to do.
ELIZABETH: Come on.
JAKE: Okay. Ready?
LAURA: Stop /

> JAKE *and* ELIZABETH *both place their hands over two identical handles on the control panel.*

ELIZABETH: Ready.
LAURA: Please / don't
JAKE: On three.
LAURA: Fuck.
JAKE: One.

> ANDREW *starts laughing.*

Two.

> LAURA *crouches and holds on tight.*

Three.

> *They press the handles in and turn them in unison.*
>
> *The pod jerks.*
>
> *Silence.*
>
> *The lights flicker out.*

2.

Two weeks earlier, in the Astro-Chamber. They record trailers.

LAURA: Hey, East Coast.
ANDREW: Hi there …
JAKE: Guten tag, Deutschland.
ELIZABETH: Hi, Kingdom of England and Wales.
LAURA: Hello.
ANDREW: … Marhabaan.
JAKE: Hola, Mexico.
ANDREW: Am I saying that right? Marhabaan?
ELIZABETH: G'day.

LAURA: Bounjour, Français! No, that means French, doesn't it? Stop trying to look smart, Laura. Fuck.

A buzzer.

Oh, sorry, swearing!

JAKE: Hi, Ireland, I'm Jake Dolan from 'Melville and Wolf: Desert Detectives'.

LAURA: I'm Laura King from Smashed Glass.

ELIZABETH: Elizabeth from 'Could Have Danced All Night'.

LAURA: I'm Laura from 'Smashed Glass'. No surname. Friendlier.

ANDREW: I'm Andrew, the voice of Jax from 'Jax and Jello'.

JAKE: And you're watching …

ELIZABETH: … and you're watching …

LAURA: … you are watching. Yes, you are. You're. You're watching …

ANDREW: … and you're watching 'Fifteen Minutes on Mars'.

LAURA: … 'Fifteen Minutes on Mars'.

ELIZABETH: … 'Fifteen Minutes on Mars'.

JAKE: 'Fifteen Minutes on Mars' on Channel Four.

ANDREW: On CBC.

ELIZABETH: Canal de las Estrellas.

LAURA: France 4.

JAKE: TVNZ.

ELIZABETH: On Italia 1.

ANDREW: On MBC.

JAKE: G'day, Australia, I'm Jake Dolan from 'Melville and Wolf: Desert Detectives' and you're watching 'Fifteen Minutes on Mars' on Channel Seven.

3.

The rec room. A large table. LAURA, ELIZABETH *and* ANDREW *sit playing cards. There is an empty space at the table where* JAKE*'s cards are. They are using their meal pills as chips. There's a small pile of pills in the centre of the table.* ELIZABETH *sorts through the pills in her hand before placing one in the centre.*

ELIZABETH: Okay. Egg and chips.

LAURA: I love egg and chips.

ELIZABETH: Could be yours.

ACT ONE

LAURA: Where's Jake?
ANDREW: He wandered off.
ELIZABETH: Because you took so long deciding.
ANDREW: It's a big decision.
LAURA: [*towards offstage*] Jake?
ELIZABETH: [*towards offstage*] It's your turn.
JAKE: [*offstage*] What?
LAURA: [*towards offstage*] It's your turn.
JAKE: [*offstage*] Sorry.

He enters holding a large manual.

LAURA: What's that?
JAKE: Manual, for the ship. I could hear something beeping.
ELIZABETH: It's your turn.
JAKE: Yeah. Where are we?
ELIZABETH: I just put down egg and chips.
JAKE: Right.

He looks at his cards.

LAURA: Beeping? Like beeping in a bad way?
JAKE: No, I don't think so.
LAURA: What does the manual say?
JAKE: It's pretty dense.
ELIZABETH: Egg and chips.
ANDREW: It's not going to tell you anything.
LAURA: Should we ask?
JAKE: I've logged it. I'll keep looking.
ELIZABETH: Jake.
JAKE: Okay. I see your egg and chips and I raise you one roast dinner.

He throws a pill into the centre of the table.

ELIZABETH: The big leagues.
LAURA: What flavour?

He reaches forward and picks up the pill again to look at it.

JAKE: Roast dinner, brackets chicken.
LAURA: Shit.

A buzzer.

Sorry.

JAKE: What you got, Laurs?

> LAURA *inspects the two pills she has left.*

LAURA: An orange juice and a chocolate pudding.
JAKE: Pudding's good.
LAURA: I'd prefer to eat it.
ELIZABETH: You're in or you're out.

> LAURA *considers then lays down her cards.*

LAURA: I'm out.
ELIZABETH: Andrew?

> ANDREW *considers the pills in front of him.*

ANDREW: Lamb vindaloo?
JAKE: That's acceptable.

> ANDREW *goes to throw his pill in.* ELIZABETH *stops him.*

ELIZABETH: Any sides?

> *He looks at the pill.*

ANDREW: Just rice.
ELIZABETH: No.
ANDREW: Well, it's either that or steak and kidney pie.
ELIZABETH: Who put the Brits in charge of food provisions?
JAKE: Vindaloo's great.
ELIZABETH: Fine. The curry stays.

> ANDREW *throws the pill in.*

Right. What have we got?

> *They all show their cards.* ELIZABETH *wins.*

Yes!

> *She scoops the pile of pills towards herself.* JAKE *starts pulling the cards together.*

JAKE: New round?
ANDREW: I'm out. You'll beat us into starvation.
ELIZABETH: Oh, come on. It's only the flavour pills, you can keep the nutritional ones.
ANDREW: I need the flavour.
ELIZABETH: Fine. Laura?

LAURA: I've gambled my week away already.
JAKE: I can lend you something.
LAURA: Nah. I'll develop a habit.
ELIZABETH: [*to* JAKE] Just you and me then.
LAURA: Do you think the other pods are more entertaining than this?

JAKE notices something. He points towards the corner of the ceiling.

JAKE: There.
LAURA: What?
JAKE: See, Laurs. I told you.

She looks.

LAURA: Oh, yeah.
JAKE: All of them.

He points around the room.

ELIZABETH: What?
JAKE: The cameras. They're not recording.
ELIZABETH: Don't be stupid.
JAKE: The red light is gone. See? All of them.
ELIZABETH: That doesn't mean anything.
ANDREW: They're filming all the time.
JAKE: I don't think so. I think it switches off, drops out sometimes.
LAURA: Fuck.
ELIZABETH: How can we know?
JAKE: No buzzer. She swore, but no buzzer.
LAURA: Fuck!

They wait. Nothing.

   Oh, my god.
ANDREW: What if they just want us to think they're not watching?

The red light comes back on the cameras.

JAKE: It's back. Act normal.
ELIZABETH: Shit.

A buzzer.

4.

LAURA *sits in the Astro-Chamber. A female voice gives her a new directive.*

VOICE: Hello, Laura. Welcome back to the Astro-Chamber. The public have spoken and this week they would like more romance. Smile to hear your challenge.

> *She smiles.*

Welcome to the romance challenge. Your target is fellow explorer and Aussie cutie Jake Dolan. Your goal is to make him starry-eyed. You can achieve your goal by any means necessary, but you must use this key phrase: 'You could be the last person I ever see'. You have until the end of the week to become star-crossed lovers. As always, if you are successful you will receive an out-of-this-world bonus of ten thousand dollars. Blow a kiss to accept this challenge.

> *She blows a kiss to the screen.*

Challenge accepted. Good luck, Laura, and remember, by any means necessary.

> *Pause.*

LAURA: Okay. You could be the last person I ever see. You could be the last person I ever see.

> *She repeats, trying different intonations until she's satisfied.*

5.

In the rec room, JAKE *is reading the manual.* ANDREW *is playing cards.*

ANDREW: It won't tell you anything.
JAKE: You said.
ANDREW: Especially not about cameras.
JAKE: I just want to know if something's broken.
ANDREW: We're the guinea pigs.
JAKE: It's a TV show, not a science experiment.
ANDREW: I'm not talking about the show. The show's just a cog in the machine.

JAKE: What machine?
ANDREW: The network owns the show. Who do you think owns the network?
JAKE: Who?
ANDREW: NASA.

    JAKE *laughs.*

JAKE: Okay.
ANDREW: It's not funny.
JAKE: Why / would
ANDREW: We're shipping out.
JAKE: We've shipped.
ANDREW: We're just the start.
JAKE: I don't think / that
ANDREW: There're more asteroids, you know.
JAKE: What?
ANDREW: Falling all the time.
JAKE: Yeah, I read the news. There's been a couple.
ANDREW: More than that. The sky's falling in.
JAKE: I really don't think / that's
ANDREW: Sinkholes too. Opening up all over.
JAKE: Yeah, I know.
ANDREW: You only know what they've told you.
JAKE: Okay.
ANDREW: The disaster drip-feed. Things are escalating a lot quicker than you think.
JAKE: There was that one sinkhole / in
ANDREW: There are hundreds of them.
JAKE: Come on.
ANDREW: Whole villages.
JAKE: Where?
ANDREW: They're in the places that don't get reported on.
JAKE: That's convenient. You really don't think it would be in the news? Hundreds of people dying?
ANDREW: Depends on the people.
JAKE: It's gone again. The red light.
ANDREW: What do you think happened to Hawaii?
JAKE: That was a tsunami. Look.

He points at the cameras. ANDREW *ignores him.*

ANDREW: Cover-up. Tsunamis don't swallow islands.

JAKE: Hawaii didn't get swallowed. It's still there, behind the wall. Just everyone died.

ANDREW: Vanished.

JAKE: Hawaii is still there.

ANDREW: Is it?

JAKE: I gave a hundred bucks to the appeal.

ANDREW: Did you?

JAKE: You're freaking me out.

ANDREW: They need a test mission.

JAKE: Why us?

ANDREW: People vote for us. Voting costs money. They need money to build the ships.

JAKE: You think the money from this show is going to go into what? A mass exodus?

ANDREW: Well, not for everyone. Just the people that can afford it.

JAKE: Don't start saying this in front of the girls.

ANDREW: So chivalrous.

JAKE: There's no point scaring people.

ANDREW: Why do you think they split the pods up? Only four people in each.

JAKE: Smaller pods, faster journey.

ANDREW: They don't want all their eggs in one basket.

6.

ELIZABETH *and* LAURA *in the Inner Sanctum.*

LAURA: Our third album was called 'Intergalactic Matriarchy' and on the cover I was wearing a t-shirt that said 'World's Top Astronaut'. Isn't that funny? The doll of me wore that t-shirt too.

ELIZABETH: Did it look like you?

LAURA: Its boobs were bigger.

VOICE: Laura and Elizabeth, welcome to the Inner Sanctum. It's important to the public that they see the fragility beneath your tough exteriors. So it's time to make yourselves vulnerable. Please begin.

ELIZABETH: You want to start?

ACT ONE

LAURA: Okay ... I had a pretty hard childhood. My mum struggled to find work so we never had any money. And she drank so ...
ELIZABETH: My mother forced me into ballet when I was three.
LAURA: Wow, that's so young.

A buzzer.

Sorry.

Pause.

Wow, ballet lessons, I feel so sorry for you.
ELIZABETH: Six days a week. Do you know how much those shoes make your feet bleed?
LAURA: Well, my feet bled too, from walking over my mum's broken vodka bottles. She would go on these benders and we'd barely see her for days.
ELIZABETH: My mum would beat me if I didn't get the steps right. I couldn't sleep I was so scared. I fantasised about quitting, about running away.
LAURA: When I got a record deal, the only thing my mum asked was how much money I'd be able to give her.
ELIZABETH: At least you could leave. I was trapped. Even when I got injured and could barely walk.
LAURA: So what? You got to quit, didn't you?
ELIZABETH: Ballet was the only thing I was good at. I never finished school. Injury isn't quitting, it's death.
LAURA: I actually wanted my career. I worked really hard for everything I got and then all it took was one unsuccessful album and they dropped us. One. Out of four.
ELIZABETH: She gave me painkillers to push through the injury. Told me to take as many as I needed to make it work.
LAURA: I had to move back to my hometown.
ELIZABETH: I lost six years of my life to those painkillers.
LAURA: I was going out every night.
ELIZABETH: I started having panic attacks.
LAURA: Taking anything I could get my hands on.
ELIZABETH: I was scared to leave the house.
LAURA: I thought about killing myself all the time.

    LAURA *bursts into tears.*

A ping.

VOICE: Thank you.
ELIZABETH: You okay?

LAURA is fine almost instantly.

LAURA: Yep.
VOICE: Thank you. You may leave.
LAURA: Have you had any challenges yet?
ELIZABETH: We're not supposed to talk about it.
LAURA: What if you don't complete a challenge?
ELIZABETH: Then you don't get the money.
LAURA: And you get voted off.
ELIZABETH: Probably.
LAURA: I can't go into isolation.
ELIZABETH: Then do the challenge.

7.

They each separately record video clips in the Astro-Chamber. They have been asked: 'What are you most looking forward to about getting HOME?'

ELIZABETH: I suppose I'm interested to see what it's like and /

A buzzer.

Sorry. The thing I'm most looking forward to about getting HOME is seeing Mars for the first time. So far away from everything. A fresh start for me and my daughter.

A ping.

JAKE: Getting home? Well … I guess my family, but /

A buzzer.

Sorry. I would be excited to get home because I really can't wait to see my family /

A buzzer.

I did it as a sentence!

A buzzer.

Oh, fuck.

ACT ONE

A buzzer.

Sorry. Yes, you don't mean home, you mean HOME. Right. I'm most looking forward to getting to our Hospitality and Operational Mars Encampment, HOME, because I can't wait to have a real adventure in space.

A ping.

ANDREW: I'm looking forward to getting HOME because …

Pause.

A buzzer.

I'm thinking.

A buzzer.

What do you want me to say? You just tell me what would help and /

A buzzer.

Okay. I'm looking forward to getting HOME because I want to contribute to the scientific study of human survival in space.

Pause. ANDREW *waits.*

A ping.

LAURA: I'm looking forward to getting HOME because I can't wait to pioneer female life on Mars and inspire other women and girls to become astronauts and space explorers too.

A ping.

8.

ANDREW *is performing a puppet show for the others. He has a red sock for* JAX *(a dog) and a purple sock for* JELLO *(a sea lion).*

JELLO: I can't believe you fought that dragon all by yourself, Jax!
JAX: I'd do anything to protect you, Jello.
JELLO: Oh, Jax, you're my hero!
JAX: Thank you, Jello. I'm the happiest dog in the land.

JAX barks. JELLO *joins in with some sea lion barks.*

JELLO: Look at that beautiful sunset.
JAX: It's almost as beautiful as you, Jello.

JELLO: Thank you, Jax. A beautiful sea lion and her brave dog. We just make the perfect couple.
JAX: The perfect couple.
JELLO: And this is the perfect end to a perfect day.
JAX: Jello, I hope we'll always be together.
JELLO: We will, Jax. We will.

> *They share a chaste kiss.*
>
> JAX *and* JELLO *bow.* ANDREW *bows.*
>
> *The others applaud.*

9.

LAURA *and* ANDREW *in the rec room.*

LAURA: I see what you're saying, but we're not exactly going to be out on the surface building shelters. The station's already set up.
ANDREW: It's about more than just surviving. It's enjoyment, relaxation, luxury. Mars is the next great destination. Lavish apartments, spa facilities, entertainment centres.
LAURA: A resort?
ANDREW: An exclusive utopia, beyond the stars.
LAURA: You sound like PR.
ANDREW: They needed people of a certain sensibility.
LAURA: Famous people?
ANDREW: We might not like it. They might not like it.
LAURA: They …? What am I supposed to know?
ANDREW: Look. You don't think this is just a TV show, do you?

> *A beeping starts.* LAURA *looks up.*

LAURA: Is that the beeping Jake was talking about?
ANDREW: I don't know.
LAURA: Does that sound bad to you?

> JAKE *enters.*

[*To* JAKE] Is this the beeping from before?
JAKE: How long's it been doing that?
LAURA: Just started.
JAKE: It's louder. I'll log it.

LAURA: Their replies take so long. I don't like this.
JAKE: The cameras are off too.
LAURA: You think it's connected?
JAKE: I'll look in the manual.
LAURA: It's a spaceship not a washing machine.

> ELIZABETH *enters.*

[*To* ELIZABETH] It's doing it again.
JAKE: Cameras are back.

> LAURA *moves to various parts of the room trying to locate the source.*

ANDREW: It's an alarm.
ELIZABETH: Where's it coming from?
LAURA: We don't fucking know. If we knew where it was fucking coming from we'd fucking know what it was.

> *A buzzer.*

Oh, fuck you.

> *A buzzer.*

ELIZABETH: Alright. I'm sure / it's
LAURA: Why am I the only one worried about this?

> *The beeping stops.*

ELIZABETH: There.

> LAURA *stares at the other three. They wait.*

VOICE: Andrew to the Astro-Chamber.

> ANDREW *exits.*

LAURA: Cameras cutting in and out, unexplained alarms.
JAKE: I'll protect you.
LAURA: I'm a strong, independent woman.
JAKE: Totally.
LAURA: I feel like I'm going crazy.
JAKE: We need some entertainment. You could sing.
LAURA: No.
JAKE: Go on.
LAURA: Which song?
JAKE: 'Work With Me'?

LAURA: 'Work *For* Me'. Call yourself a fan?
JAKE: I remember the video.
LAURA: I think you missed the point of the song.
JAKE: Maybe if you sing it I'll get it this time.
LAURA: [*to* ELIZABETH] Did you ever watch Jake's show?
ELIZABETH: I missed it.
LAURA: Him and his dog were the cutest little private detectives.
JAKE: Cool, funny, badass private detectives.
LAURA: Was the dog called Wolf in real life?
JAKE: No. Lucy, Bertie and Alice.
LAURA: Wow. TV.

The beeping starts again.

Fuck.

A buzzer.

ELIZABETH: Maybe it's a test.
LAURA: How do you think we're doing?

10.

ELIZABETH *in the Astro-Chamber.*

ELIZABETH: What will I miss most about life on Earth? Well, I'll miss … nature. Yes. I'll be sad not to see trees and flowers, to not be able to share them with my daughter.

Pause. She waits for a response.

Is that okay? Can I go?

Pause.

Are you there? [*Realising*] The light's not on. Can you hear me?

She tests it.

Fuck.

She waits for a buzzer, doesn't get one.

What the fuck am I doing? Fuck. Fuck, what the fuck am I doing? A baby. A fucking baby. I can't have a fucking baby in space. Fucking hell. I just want it gone. I want it gone. I want it gone. Fuck. Fuck. Fuck. Fuck.

A buzzer.

She looks up suddenly.

Hello?

11.

They are all in the rec room, sitting around the table playing cards. They play in silence for a while, throwing pills in the middle, not bothering to call out what they're betting with.

LAURA: This is boring.

ELIZABETH: Want to raise the stakes?

LAURA: No, I mean we're being boring. For the viewers. We need to amp this up.

JAKE: Strip poker.

LAURA: No way.

ELIZABETH: It's the producer's job to amp it up, not ours.

LAURA: They could cancel our pod.

ELIZABETH: No they couldn't.

JAKE: I'm just saying, getting naked is guaranteed ratings.

LAURA: We just spent seven months asleep. I need time to get toned up.

JAKE: How long are we talking?

LAURA: Mars better have a good gym.

ELIZABETH: Relax.

LAURA: Excuse me for wanting to be entertaining.

ELIZABETH: The cameras aren't even on.

LAURA: What? [*Looking*] Fuck. But it's not beeping.

JAKE: Yeah, I'm not sure those are connected.

LAURA: So what does the beeping mean?

JAKE: Never got an answer.

LAURA: Fuck.

ELIZABETH: You can stop trying so hard.

LAURA: I have to try hard. I'm the sexy fun one!

ELIZABETH: Sure.

    LAURA *screams.*

    They all stare at her.

LAURA: Sorry. I've just been wanting to do that for so long.

They burst out laughing.

Pause.

ELIZABETH *screams. Then* JAKE. *Then* ANDREW. *Then* LAURA *again. They scream together.*

Pause.

JAKE: How are we gonna last a year?
LAURA: I have no idea.
ELIZABETH: It's back on.
VOICE: Laura and Elizabeth to the Inner Sanctum.
JAKE: Laurs, you wanna talk training schedules later?

LAURA *shoots him a look.* LAURA *and* ELIZABETH *leave.*

Pause.

ANDREW: You don't really think the cameras are switching off, do you?

Pause.

JAKE: I don't know what you mean.

12.

In the Astro-Chamber. The voice gives JAKE *a directive.*

VOICE: Hello, Jake. You are now just one day from HOME, the Hospitality and Operational Mars Encampment, we hope you're excited! And if that wasn't enough, we have some awesome news: The public has voted and they have a new challenge for you. Flex to hear your challenge.

He flexes his bicep.

Welcome to the hero challenge. The public has decided that you, Jake Dolan, will be our hero.

This is one of the most difficult challenges we have, but we know you can do it. Upon completion you will receive a hero-worthy bonus of 50,000 dollars.

There can only be one hero. And you must use this key phrase: 'This is something I have to do'.

You'll know when the time has come to step up to your destiny. This is the role you were always intended for, so no matter what, you must fulfill your duties.

ACT ONE 19

Fist pump to accept this challenge.

He fist pumps.

Challenge accepted. Good luck, Jake. When crisis strikes, you'll know what to do. And remember, there can only be one hero.

JAKE: Cool. Great. This is something I have to do.

13.

ELIZABETH *and* ANDREW *in the Inner Sanctum.*

VOICE: Elizabeth and Andrew, welcome to the Inner Sanctum. The public have noticed a rising tension between you and would like you to assassinate each other's characters. Please begin.

ELIZABETH: This should be easy.

ANDREW: Ready?

ELIZABETH: Yeah. No, wait. Why did your ex-wife leave you again?

ANDREW: For another puppeteer on the show.

ELIZABETH: Oh yeah, a fox, right?

ANDREW: Right.

ELIZABETH: Okay, ready.

VOICE: Please begin.

ANDREW: So I don't get your casting here. You're meant to be the perfect mother and the bitch?

ELIZABETH: Women can be more than one thing, you know.

ANDREW: Confusing messaging.

A buzzer. This is tame.

ELIZABETH: Start again.

ANDREW: Okay. So you're supposed to be a perfect mother and a heinous bitch?

ELIZABETH: Just like your mum.

ANDREW: My mum is really nice actually.

A buzzer.

Sorry. You go.

ELIZABETH: Raising a creepy loner, I bet she's so proud.

ANDREW: Well, you're really nailing one half of your personality today.

ELIZABETH: Alright, conspiracy geek, why don't you go jerk off into your tin foil hat?

ANDREW: I feel sorry for your baby. Its mother's a failed ballerina, failed dancing show judge and now a failed reality star too.

ELIZABETH: I'm the failure? Everyone's betting on your mental breakdown before we even land.

ANDREW: At least I got here on talent instead of using my child as a biology experiment.

ELIZABETH: At least my wife didn't get off on fucking fox puppets.

Pause.

ANDREW *bursts out laughing.* ELIZABETH *joins in. They can't stop laughing.*

A buzzer.

ANDREW: Sorry. Sorry!

ELIZABETH: Okay okay, let's pull this together.

ANDREW: That was gross.

ELIZABETH: I was in the moment!

A buzzer.

ANDREW: Time to go nuclear?

ELIZABETH: Agreed.

ANDREW: Ready?

ELIZABETH: Ready.

ANDREW: Why don't you just throw yourself out an airlock right now, you dried-up, drug-addict bitch?

ELIZABETH *slaps him across the face.*

A ping.

14.

JAKE *and* LAURA *in the rec room.*

JAKE: I like her.

LAURA: Who?

JAKE: Astro-lady. She flirts with me a bit.

LAURA: She's not real.

JAKE: Bit prejudiced.

LAURA: She's just a computer.

JAKE: A computer who knows how to talk.

LAURA: My hairdryer knows how to talk.
JAKE: Such authority. 'Jake, go here.' 'Jake, answer this.'
LAURA: Stop perving on the machines.
JAKE: Are you jealous?
LAURA: Should I be?

Pause.

JAKE: Got a message from my mum. My little brother's been picked for the under tens.
LAURA: In what?
JAKE: Football. Aussie rules.
LAURA: Is that what you call soccer?
JAKE: No, soccer's what we call soccer.
LAURA: So what's football?
JAKE: Football's football.
LAURA: Never mind.

Pause. LAURA *grasps for conversation.*

So … how old is he?
JAKE: Eight. He's my half-brother. Xavier.
LAURA: Xavier. Good name.
JAKE: He's gonna go pro.
LAURA: That's cute. You must miss him.
JAKE: Yeah. It's weird, it feels like we've been gone forever, but also only like a couple of days.
LAURA: Did you know Mars days are longer? Twenty-four hours and forty minutes.
JAKE: So we're going slower than Earth?
LAURA: Yeah, every day they get a little bit further ahead of us.
JAKE: Mind fuck.

Pause.

LAURA: Do you think we'll ever go back?
JAKE: Of course. When the show's over.
LAURA: But anything could happen up here.
JAKE: Anything could happen down there.

Pause. They get closer.

LAURA: Jake?

JAKE: Yeah?
LAURA: Do you ever think …?
JAKE: What?
LAURA: Well, if something happens … It's nothing.

> *She gets a lot closer to him. He glances at the camera.*

JAKE: The light's on.
LAURA: What?
JAKE: The cameras …
LAURA: So?
JAKE: Don't you think we should wait till they …
LAURA: I can't wait.

> *He goes in to kiss her but she remembers she hasn't said the line and pulls away.*

Jake?
JAKE: Yeah?
LAURA: You could be the last person I ever see.

> *They kiss uncontrollably.*

15.

They each separately record video clips in the Astro-Chamber. They have been asked: What are your fears for this trip?

ELIZABETH: My biggest fear? I've got so many. I just want a good future for my daughter.

> *A ping.*

JAKE: My biggest fear is disappointing my family.

> *A ping.*

ANDREW: …

> *A buzzer.*
>
> *A buzzer.*
>
> *A buzzer.*
>
> *A buzzer.*
>
> *A buzzer.*

LAURA: My biggest fear is that we do this, we land on Mars, live there, complete our challenges and people watch us, and it's a success, you know. And then we go home. We go home and it all lasts a little bit longer, but then, in a year, the new people get here. And they're funnier than us, better looking, more charismatic, more daring, more famous even. The figures shoot up, the rewards, the endorsement deals and soon. Well. And soon no-one even remembers us. Soon we're just the bad first series.

A buzzer.

16.

Back to the beginning.

LAURA: Jake, don't be a fucking hero!
JAKE: What?
LAURA: Just / don't
JAKE: We haven't got time to discuss this. Liz, you take that side.
ELIZABETH: Got it.

They position themselves.

LAURA: Jake. Please. I'm begging / you
JAKE: I'm sorry.
LAURA: Please /
JAKE: Laura. This is something I have to do.
ELIZABETH: Come on.
JAKE: Okay. Ready?
LAURA: Stop /

JAKE and ELIZABETH both place their hands over two identical handles on the control panel.

ELIZABETH: Ready.
LAURA: Please / don't
JAKE: On three.
LAURA: Fuck.
JAKE: One.

ANDREW starts laughing.

Two.

> LAURA *crouches and holds on tight.*

Three.

> *They press the handles in and turn them in unison.*
>
> *The pod jerks.*
>
> *Silence.*
>
> *The lights flicker out.*

Is everyone okay?

ELIZABETH: Yes.

LAURA: Yeah.

JAKE: Andrew?

ANDREW: Yes.

JAKE: Okay. We need to try to get the lights back on. Liz, are you still by the control panel?

ELIZABETH: Yes, but I can't see what anything is.

JAKE: Let's just start from the bottom and work our way up.

> *He starts pressing everything on the panel.*

LAURA: Oh, my god.

ELIZABETH: Are you sure?

JAKE: What else can we do?

> ELIZABETH *starts pressing too.*

LAURA: You can't just randomly press buttons. You don't have a fucking clue /

> *The beeping starts.*

Fuck!

JAKE: Okay, can anyone remember any controls on the panel?

ELIZABETH: Yes. Yes. The brakes were next to the override.

JAKE: Good.

LAURA: I can't tell if we're still moving.

JAKE: Have you got it?

ELIZABETH: Yes.

LAURA: What is that?

JAKE: What?

> *An alarm starts ringing. The beeping continues simultaneously.*

ACT ONE

LAURA: Look /

She points out of the window of the pod.

ELIZABETH: Oh, my / god
JAKE: It's one of the other / pods
LAURA: Fuck /
ELIZABETH: They're coming right at / us
LAURA: I can't see the / surface
ELIZABETH: We're going the wrong / way

The lights come back on. ELIZABETH *has her hand on a lever.*

JAKE: Get the brakes /
ELIZABETH: Which / way
JAKE: I'll do it /
LAURA: Jake, you don't know what / you're

JAKE *takes the lever.*

ELIZABETH: We're gonna crash into / them

ANDREW *laughs manically.*

LAURA: Fuck /
ELIZABETH: Do something /
LAURA: Jake /
JAKE: I can do this. I can do this.

He pulls the lever back.

The pod jerks forward, accelerating.

JAKE *and* ELIZABETH *both frantically scramble for the lever.*

LAURA *screams.*

A deafening explosion.

Blackout.

END OF ACT ONE

ACT TWO

1.

Twenty years later.

The Museum of Childhood, Melbourne.

Occasionally the image glitches, as though we are watching through a faulty video feed.

A phone rings. A message cuts in.

MESSAGE: Thank you for contacting the Museum of Childhood. We keep your memories safe, so you don't have to. To hear our opening times, ticket prices and visitor experience data, think one. To speak with our enhanced linguistic comm-droids, think two. To speak with our service-professional humans, think three.

    A glitch.

2.

The Museum's front of house.

CAROLINE: I hate the amount she contacts me. And how she contacts me. And what she says. And how sometimes I won't hear from her for ages—like it's a trap. And I hate her disappointed voice. And when she pretends to be more excited about something I'm telling her than she really is. I hate that she can't process my way of life. I hate how she thinks I haven't achieved. And how guilty she makes me feel. And those shit presents she buys. And how much she talks about my sister. And the glowing way my sister talks about her. And how they interface with each other. I hate the judgement in her voice. And how annoyed she gets. And her pride. And how she thinks I always ruin a special occasion.

    Pause.

Yeah, I'd delete all of that.

ACT TWO

NICKI: It doesn't work like that.
CAROLINE: I know how it works. I'm just talking.
NICKI: I'm trying to work.
CAROLINE: What about your mum? Wouldn't it just be perfect? To just press delete?
NICKI: I was fostered.
CAROLINE: What about your daughter?
NICKI: I wouldn't undo anything.
CAROLINE: Goody two shoes.

A glitch.

3.

NICKI: Have you seen Ellie?
CAROLINE: No.

A glitch.

NICKI: Have you seen Ellie?
CAROLINE: No.

A glitch.

NICKI: Have you seen Ellie?
CAROLINE: No.

A glitch.

4.

A phone call. NICKI *doesn't talk, she operates recordings of her own voice, selecting appropriate answers.*

NICKI: Thank you for contacting the Museum of Childhood. We keep your memories safe, so you don't have to. Nicki speaking.
   Hello, Daniel.
   Yes, the Museum is open seven days a week from ten a.m. to five p.m.
   Yes, we have a record of all Australian citizens.
   Yes.
   Are you an Australian citizen?
   Perfect, then we'll have your record.

Absolutely. The Museum of Childhood is part of the Memory Database Centralisation Initiative, allowing all citizens to back up their data accessibly and affordably. We don't want the rising cost of data storage to impair your memories.

That's right.

Yes.

Yes, the Museum collates CCTV footage, flight, passport and travel card records, media coverage and online activity, as well as all user-provided materials, to create a unique, interfacial exhibit of your own personal history.

Of course.

Citizens who wish to maintain private storage can back up their memories externally, however the Centralisation Initiative is the only free national storage system. Your data is stored automatically, but you have the choice whether to view and add to your record.

No, we don't charge you to store your record, you only have to pay to view it.

Yes.

I'm sure, yes.

No, you don't have to make that decision right away.

You're welcome.

Would you like me to schedule you in?

Of course, no problem.

Yes.

Yes, I have seen the Museum's record of my childhood. It was wonderful. I'd definitely recommend it to others.

You're welcome.

Thank you for contacting the Museum of Childhood, Daniel. 'Bye 'bye.

A glitch.

5.

CAROLINE: Do you think they fired her?
NICKI: I don't know.
CAROLINE: I've heard rumours.
NICKI: So have I.

CAROLINE: They located something in her record.
NICKI: That's what I heard.
CAROLINE: What?
NICKI: I don't know.
CAROLINE: Do you think her replacement will be one of them?
NICKI: No.
CAROLINE: Why not?
NICKI: They tried before. Before you started.
CAROLINE: What happened?
NICKI: Its face kept peeling off.
CAROLINE: Things have come a long way.
NICKI: Not that far.
CAROLINE: They have no past. There's nothing to locate.
NICKI: And they're cheaper.
CAROLINE: Yes.
NICKI: But unreliable.
CAROLINE: My sister has a nanny. She's called Bluebell. She smiles all the time.
NICKI: You can't trust them.
CAROLINE: The comm-droids aren't as sophisticated as the nanny models. They're like a vending machine that talks. Not even psychic-enabled. You practically have to oil the limbs.
NICKI: I don't want them anywhere near me.
CAROLINE: They're coming whether you like it or not.

A glitch.

6.

ALEX *is there.*

NICKI: He looks so …
CAROLINE: Yeah.
ALEX: Hello. My name's Alex.
NICKI: And sounds …
CAROLINE: Yeah.
NICKI: Fuck.
ALEX: You are my employees at the Museum of Childhood. I'm pleased to meet you. I hope you're having a lovely day.

NICKI: The old one was not like this.
CAROLINE: Must be an update.
NICKI: Touch it.
CAROLINE: You're not supposed to touch them.
NICKI: Not officially.

> CAROLINE *hesitantly picks up a pen and gently pokes* ALEX's *arm with it.*

ALEX: That's my arm.
NICKI: What does it feel like?
CAROLINE: Weird. I've never touched one before.
NICKI: Give it here.

> CAROLINE *hands* NICKI *the pen.* NICKI *stabs it hard into* ALEX's *arm so it lodges in there.*

CAROLINE: Fuck.
ALEX: That's my arm.
CAROLINE: What are you doing?
NICKI: Just checking he's not human.

> ALEX *pulls the pen out and offers it to* NICKI.

ALEX: Did you drop your pen?
NICKI: Fuck.

> *A glitch.*

7.

A phone call. ALEX's *mouth hangs open. His recordings play from it.*

ALEX: Only you have open access to your record.
You are able to nominate up to two people who can view your record independently.
You may also nominate someone to inherit your record after you die.
If you die intestate, your record will go to your next of kin.
Yes, your wife.
After that your oldest child.
After that your youngest child.
After that your parents.

After that your siblings.
After that your grandchildren.
After that your grandparents.
After that your best friend.
After that your nieces or nephews.
After that your aunts or uncles.
After that your great-grandchildren.
After that your second-best friend.
After that your great-grandparents.
After that your first cousins.
After that your third-best friend.
After that your closest colleague.
After that your line manager.
After that your great-great-grandchildren.
After that your first cousin once removed.
After that your next-door neighbour.
After that your best friend's child.
After that your best friend's grandchild.
After that your first cousin twice removed.
After that your second cousin once removed.
After that your third cousin thrice removed.
After that your fourth-best friend.

Pause.

No, you may not delete your record.

A glitch.

8.

NICKI: She slept right through it.
CAROLINE: Who did?
NICKI: Isabelle.
CAROLINE: Through what?
NICKI: The explosions.
CAROLINE: When?
NICKI: Last night.
ALEX: Fourteen.
CAROLINE: Explosions?

ALEX: Dead.
CAROLINE: I must have slept through it too.

Something beeps.

Pod five. Trauma rating.
NICKI: How high?
CAROLINE: Seven.
NICKI: They were loud, the explosions. I think it's getting worse.
CAROLINE: I should riot more. You know, while I'm young.
NICKI: I used to.
CAROLINE: Your dark past.
NICKI: Pre-motherhood.
CAROLINE: Do you riot, Alex?
ALEX: Violence is against our core principles.
CAROLINE: You've got nothing to feel angry about.
ALEX: Thank you.

Something beeps.

CAROLINE: Eight.
NICKI: Wait till nine.
CAROLINE: Sure.
NICKI: She's just so used to it.
CAROLINE: Who is?
NICKI: Isabelle.
CAROLINE: I had a really good sleep actually. I woke up feeling completely rested.
NICKI: I go to her room to see if she's upset and she's always totally shut down. I get into bed with her, in case she wakes up, but she never does. When I was her age I still slept with the light on.
ALEX: Isabelle. Searching.
NICKI: What are you doing?
ALEX: Daughter. Four years old.
NICKI: Don't view my daughter.
CAROLINE: I felt like I'd slept for days. Completely rebooted.
ALEX: Isabelle has a record.
NICKI: I can't afford private storage, doesn't mean you can just look her up.
ALEX: I have access to all records.

CAROLINE: I heard that we update every cell in our body every seven years, is that true? All of my cells feel /

Something beeps.

Nine.

NICKI: You go.

CAROLINE: I went last time.

NICKI: Alex?

A glitch.

9.

XAVIER *in the Museum.*

He wears a headset that covers his eyes. We can't see what he is seeing but the sound of the recordings pumps through the room. Each time he turns, a new memory plays. The memories start to overlap. He gets increasingly agitated.

AUDIO: Happy birthday, mate! Here you go.

Wow, look at that! What do you say to your brother?

The production company are refusing to take responsibility for what they are calling a tragic and unforeseen accident.

Go on, Xav! Get the ball! Kick it! Yeeeeesssss!

We just want justice for our son, so our family can begin to move on.

Wolf! Look at these footprints. Get the scent, boy, get the scent. Yeah! Come on! Come on, Wolf! Let's catch him!

Closer! Move in closer. Xav, cuddle up to your brother. That's right. Jake, put your arm around him. That's right. Great. Say happy Christmas!

There he is, there he is. Look, your brother's on TV again! Are you recording this? Are you getting it?

[*Sung*] Join our adventure and have some fun
    Under the shining desert sun.
    Mystery, intrigue, sometimes danger,
    Who goes there? Friend or stranger?
    A plucky young Holmes and his four-legged Watson,
    They'll crack the case, long before the cops can,

Whatever the crime they're fast and effective, 'Melville and Wolf: Desert Detectives'!

XAVIER *tears the headset off and throws it to the ground.*

A glitch.

10.

Their voice recordings play.

NICKI: Yes, I have seen the Museum's record of my childhood. It was wonderful.
CAROLINE: It was wonderful.
ALEX: Yes. I have seen the Museum's record of my childhood.
NICKI: It was wonderful. I'd definitely recommend it to others.
CAROLINE: I'd definitely recommend it to others.
NICKI: It was wonderful. I'd definitely /
ALEX: Yes, I have seen /
CAROLINE: I'd definitely recommend /
ALEX: It was /
NICKI: My childhood. It was /
CAROLINE: Definitely /
ALEX: Wonderful /
NICKI: I'd /
ALEX: Yes /
NICKI: Recommend it /
CAROLINE: Yes, I have /
ALEX: My childhood /
NICKI: Was wonderful /
CAROLINE: I'd definitely recommend /
NICKI: Record of my childhood /
ALEX: Wonderful /
CAROLINE: Wonderful /
NICKI: Wonderful /
ALL: I'd definitely recommend it to others.

A glitch.

11.

CAROLINE: If
   We
   Talk
   Really
   Slowly
   He
   Can't
   Process
   Us.
NICKI: Really?
CAROLINE: Isn't
   That
   Right
   Alex?
ALEX: Can't process. Please repeat.
NICKI: Whataboutifwetalkreallyfast?
CAROLINE: AlexcanyouprocessmewhenItalklikethis?
ALEX: Can't process. Please repeat.
NICKI: Hisbrain'stooslowtokeepupwithus.
CAROLINE: Doesn'tevenhaveabrainwehavebrainshe'sgotnothing.
NICKI: He'swiresandmetalandwe'rejellyandneuronsfiringfasterthanlight.
CAROLINE: Fasterthanlightandtwiceasbrightpewpewpew.
NICKI: Thriceasbrightpewpewpewpewpew.
CAROLINE: Ourbrainsareasbigasthegalaxyasbigastheuniverse.
NICKI: Asbigaseverythingthathaseverbeenorwilleverbe.
CAROLINE: Firingallthetimedayandnightburningbrighterandbrighterandbrighter.
NICKI: Thriceasbrightthriceasbrightthriceasbright.
CAROLINE: Brighterthanyou'lleverbebrighterthanyou'lleverbealex.
ALEX: Can't process.
NICKI: Pewpewpewpewpewalex.
ALEX: Please repeat.

CAROLINE: Pewpewpewpewpewpewpewpewpewpew.
   A glitch.

12.

XAVIER: How long have you worked here?
CAROLINE: Why?
XAVIER: I'm just curious.
CAROLINE: I don't give out personal data.
XAVIER: What's your name?
CAROLINE: Caroline.
XAVIER: Is that your real name?
CAROLINE: Sure.
XAVIER: My name's Xavier.
CAROLINE: I know. I have your record in front of me.
XAVIER: You served me the other day.
CAROLINE: Did I?
XAVIER: Don't you remember?
CAROLINE: I see a lot of people.
XAVIER: Do you ever look at people's records?
CAROLINE: Of course not.
XAVIER: You're not a stickler for the rules, are you?
CAROLINE: I respect privacy.
XAVIER: What if you fancy them?
CAROLINE: This is the Museum of Childhood.
XAVIER: I mean the adult them.
CAROLINE: I don't.
XAVIER: Fancy people?
CAROLINE: Fancy you.
XAVIER: I remember you, from the other day.
CAROLINE: I'm very distinctive.
XAVIER: You were nice to me.
CAROLINE: I'm very good at my job.
XAVIER: But you don't remember me.
CAROLINE: You have to view something six times to remember it.
XAVIER: It's three. Three times.
CAROLINE: I work in memory facilitation. It's six.
XAVIER: Our memories must be getting worse.

ACT TWO

CAROLINE: The energy has been redistributed.

XAVIER: What does that mean?

CAROLINE: We can concentrate on the present moment without worrying about what is and isn't being backed up.

XAVIER: So you're saying the past doesn't matter.

CAROLINE: I'm saying you have my full attention.

XAVIER: But only after six visits.

CAROLINE: Yes, and this is your fourth.

XAVIER: I thought / you

CAROLINE: I have your record in front of me.

XAVIER: What about memories we don't want?

CAROLINE: You can't undo the past.

XAVIER: Can't you?

CAROLINE: No.

XAVIER: What if I didn't like all of my record?

CAROLINE: You signed the waiver.

XAVIER: It is you, isn't it?

CAROLINE: You control the extent to which you interface with a memory, but the memories themselves cannot be undone.

XAVIER: You're her. You're Caroline.

CAROLINE: It's all clearly stated in the waiver. Which you signed.

XAVIER: I was given your name.

CAROLINE: By who?

XAVIER: They said you could help me. With some editing.

CAROLINE: I can't process what you're saying.

XAVIER: I need to delete part of my record.

CAROLINE: You can't delete your record.

XAVIER: I don't know how this works. Do I give you a specific time or ...?

CAROLINE: I really can't /

XAVIER: It's my brother, Jake. Jake Dolan. I want him deleted from my record. You can do that, can't you? Delete a whole person? They said you're the best.

CAROLINE: We have security here. They're good. We have to kick people out all the time.

XAVIER: He's there in every memory. Every single one. And he's dead ... so. He left ... so. I want him gone. You probably don't need my reasons. Is that enough data? I'd appreciate your help.

CAROLINE: Of course I'd prefer if you just left of your own accord.
XAVIER: I can pay. Of course, sorry, of course I can pay.
CAROLINE: I prefer it when we don't have to use force.
XAVIER: Here. [*Motioning to his pocket*] I have ... I have it with me. I don't know how you want to do this. With the cameras.
CAROLINE: Don't look at the cameras.
XAVIER: Sorry. I have it here.

    Pause.

CAROLINE: Do you love him or hate him?
XAVIER: Does it matter?
CAROLINE: Not to me.
XAVIER: It's not that I miss him. It's not that.
CAROLINE: People come in here. They want to delete their dad or their best friend or their mum or their stepsister or their uncle or whatever. Because it's too hard. But you can't switch it off.
XAVIER: It's not that.
CAROLINE: Then what?
XAVIER: I hate him.

    Pause.

CAROLINE: How much?
XAVIER: Five hundred.
CAROLINE: Double it.

    A glitch.

13.

A phone call. CAROLINE *operates her recordings.*

CAROLINE: I've processed that.
    I've processed that.
    Yes.
    I'm very sorry.
    I've processed that.
    Unfortunately company policy states that no records can be undone or deleted.
    My superior would duplicate my response. Our guidelines are very clear.

ACT TWO

Yes.

No.

I will log your complaint, however, I should inform you that to date no exceptions have been made on this policy.

Perhaps you can view the record as a memorial to your daughter.

Yes.

I've processed that.

Our strict privacy guidelines prevent me from viewing the record personally but—

Yes.

If the abduction was captured on CCTV it would be included, yes.

A shopping mall, I've processed that.

I'm very sorry.

Anything that was captured on CCTV would be—

Yes.

Yes.

Even that.

Unfortunately company policy states that no records can be undone or deleted.

No.

No.

No.

Thank you for contacting.

A glitch.

14.

CAROLINE *hacks* ALEX.

He stands up and spins around. His face is placid.

He dances.

CAROLINE *smiles.* ALEX *dances and dances.*

A glitch.

15.

CAROLINE: When did you sign the release?
NICKI: Yesterday.

CAROLINE: How long will it take them to access it?
NICKI: A few days, I suppose.
CAROLINE: Maybe it won't be in there.
NICKI: Of course it will, you know it will.
CAROLINE: How bad is it?
NICKI: It's bad.
CAROLINE: What are you going to do?
NICKI: Everything relies on her getting this scholarship. Everything. If she doesn't get it, I can't afford to pay. We'll have to move to a different catchment area. But there's nowhere affordable that's close to work and the bond on a new place / and
CAROLINE: Maybe they won't locate it.
NICKI: They'll locate it. They have computers that scan everything. Locate any small thing to use against you. It happened to a friend of mine, she had to move overseas.
CAROLINE: I'm sorry.
NICKI: Caro. You have to help me.
CAROLINE: Are you joking?
NICKI: Please.
CAROLINE: You're always telling me to stop it. That I'll get us both fired.
NICKI: I know.
CAROLINE: You wouldn't even take a cut you were so far up the moral high ground.
NICKI: I know. I'm sorry. Please. Please, I'm begging you.
CAROLINE: Fuck.
NICKI: It's not for me. It's not for me, it's for Isabelle. Please. I would never ask. I'm sorry about what I've said. I take it back. Please, do it for my daughter. For Isabelle. Izzy. Please.
CAROLINE: … Okay.
NICKI: Thank you. Thank you so much.
CAROLINE: It's okay.
NICKI: I can't afford to pay you.
CAROLINE: I know.
NICKI: Thank you. This means so much to me. I really can't thank / you
CAROLINE: You'll have to tell me what you did.
NICKI: Yes.

CAROLINE: So I can delete it.
NICKI: Of course.
CAROLINE: So ...
NICKI: It was years ago. I was only fifteen, so stupid. It's just insane how they can locate the smallest thing and just blow it up / into
CAROLINE: What did you do?
NICKI: I had a fight with another girl. Not a fight. An argument. I didn't like her. Well, she didn't like me. She had a rich family and she was calling me names. Stuff about not knowing my real parents / and
CAROLINE: So you punched her.
NICKI: No I didn't punch her. I'm not a violent person. Just, we were shouting and I pushed her. And she fell. Only, we were on the side of the road and as she fell, a car went by and it hit her.
CAROLINE: Did she die?
NICKI: She was paralysed.
CAROLINE: What's her name?
NICKI: Why?
CAROLINE: So I can search it in your record. It'll be the quickest way.
NICKI: Isla Jacobs.
CAROLINE: Okay.
NICKI: But you know I'm not like that, don't you? It was just an accident. I would never do anything to hurt anyone. I mean, I've got a daughter. You know that, don't you?

A glitch.

16.

XAVIER: You served me last week.
CAROLINE: I don't remember.
XAVIER: I remember you.
CAROLINE: I see a lot of people.
XAVIER: Xavier.
CAROLINE: It rings a bell.
XAVIER: I came to see you.
CAROLINE: Yes. Distinctive name.
XAVIER: I used to play football.
CAROLINE: That's right.
XAVIER: My brother paid for me to go to an academy.

CAROLINE: Yes.
XAVIER: I was going to go professional.
CAROLINE: Everyone told you you'd go professional.
XAVIER: Scouts watched me play every weekend.
CAROLINE: They all told you you were special. Your mum, your dad, your big brother. But then you lost all your money in the court case against the TV network. Even your brother's life insurance got swallowed up. You moved to Sydney with your mum. Stopped training. You let it all slip away. All that talent.
XAVIER: So you do remember me.
CAROLINE: You'd think to yourself: If only he hadn't gone. If it wasn't for me, if it wasn't for the money I needed for football, maybe he wouldn't be dead. You let it eat away at you. Then you found out about the conspiracy theories. The ones about the crash being faked. You spent your teenage years looking into them. Talking with weirdoes. Chasing up leads. Your mother begged you to stop.
XAVIER: I thought you didn't look at other people's records.
CAROLINE: What's a little privacy between friends?

Pause.

XAVIER: I've heard it's nice up there.
CAROLINE: Heaven?
XAVIER: Mars.
CAROLINE: You don't still believe the conspiracies, do you?
XAVIER: I've heard it's the life of luxury.
CAROLINE: My sister is going. Her wife is very rich.
XAVIER: You don't want to go too?
CAROLINE: She invented this resin. It was an accident, actually. She worked in medicine, in a lab. She was trying to make a material to repair a liver, like an organ Polyfilla. But it came out too fragile. She's advanced though, very determined. She thought she could still do something with it. Started adding colour to it, moulding it into different shapes. She mentioned it to some friends in tech.
XAVIER: What is it?
CAROLINE: They use it for their eyes, in the superior models. The resin looks wet. They look like they're looking at you.
XAVIER: If I was you, I'd go with her.
CAROLINE: Is there a reason you're here?

XAVIER: I think I made a mistake.
CAROLINE: It's too late.
XAVIER: You could get in a lot of trouble.
CAROLINE: Who are you going to tell?

A glitch.

17.

NICKI: Can you do it to Alex?
CAROLINE: Have you got a taste for it now?
NICKI: Can you?
CAROLINE: Of course I can.
NICKI: Have you done it already?
CAROLINE: Yes.
NICKI: Show me.
CAROLINE: No.
NICKI: What do you do?
CAROLINE: I make him dance.
NICKI: Show me.
CAROLINE: You don't deserve it.
NICKI: I'm grateful. For what you did.
CAROLINE: I know.
NICKI: So show me.
CAROLINE: You're a monster.

A glitch.

18.

ALEX: Welcome to the Museum of Childhood. We keep your memories safe, so you don't have to.

He resets.

Welcome to the Museum of Childhood. We keep your memories safe, so you don't have to.

He resets.

Welcome to the Museum of Childhood. We keep your memories safe, so you don't have to.

He resets.

Welcome to the Museum of Childhood. We keep your memories safe, so you don't have to.

He resets.

Welcome to the Museum of Childhood. We keep your memories safe, so you don't have to.

He resets.

Welcome to the Museum of /

NICKI *smacks him hard across the back of the head. He falls to the floor.*

A glitch.

19.

ALEX *is lying on the ground.*

NICKI: When does she go?
CAROLINE: Next week.
NICKI: How long's the journey?
CAROLINE: Seven months.
NICKI: How much?
CAROLINE: She wouldn't tell me.
NICKI: Are you jealous?
CAROLINE: No.

    Pause.

NICKI: I heard it's too hot. Airless.
CAROLINE: I heard there's no character. Everything's new so all the houses are duplicate.
NICKI: I heard they built fake trees.
CAROLINE: Fake trees?
NICKI: And flowers and hedges and grass. Everyone has their own little patch of fake grass. A home away from home.
CAROLINE: Why have we got to do that? Make everything duplicate.
NICKI: I heard there're no raised voices. Everyone argues in whispers.
CAROLINE: I heard there's no food. You download a program that feels like eating. Like a hot bacon sandwich. Like mango juice dripping down your chin.

ACT TWO

NICKI: I heard there's no more children now, that the atmosphere makes you sterile.
CAROLINE: I heard people only have sex with droids there. That they build these ideal creatures and other humans just aren't attractive anymore.
NICKI: I heard that people have been getting violent.
CAROLINE: I heard they put thirty million into building a pool, but the water kept vanishing.
NICKI: The air pressure makes people light-headed, so the slightest thing can set them off. Can turn them on their neighbours.
CAROLINE: I heard there are no guns there. And no knives.
NICKI: But your hands are a weapon.
CAROLINE: I heard the lights never go out.
NICKI: You reach out and press your fingertips into their cheek. You keep pressing until your nails pierce the skin and then your fingers pierce the flesh. I heard flesh comes away easily from the skull.
CAROLINE: I heard the ground feels like ice.
NICKI: I heard face meat tastes the sweetest. The blood dripping down your chin.
CAROLINE: I heard everyone went blind.
NICKI: I heard it's wonderful.
CAROLINE: I wish I could see it.
NICKI: So do I.

Pause.

CAROLINE: I think they know.
NICKI: About what?
CAROLINE: Everything.
NICKI: I thought you were careful.
CAROLINE: I was.
NICKI: What will you do?
CAROLINE: I don't know.
NICKI: I can't lose this job.
CAROLINE: What have you ever done for me?

A glitch.

20.

CAROLINE *is gone.*

NICKI: Do you like dancing, Alex?
ALEX: I have no purpose for dancing.
NICKI: But do you like it?
ALEX: I can list each individual form of dance.
> Or tell you how and where the forms originated.
> Or find an instructional video on how to dance.
> Or play you songs to dance to.
> Or a tutorial on the manipulation of limbs.
> Or give reasons why dance may be enjoyable.
> Or an overview of influential dancers through the ages.
> Or the best places to go to dance.
> Or to learn to dance.
> Or to watch dancing.
> Or find a dance class for you to attend.
> Or tell you the way hips sway to a rhythm.
> Or tell you the way a human neck curves and bends.
> Or select the particular utterances of your arms and legs.
> Or the puffy opening of your mouth.
> Or the shake of your skin.
> Or the exposure of your spine.
> Or perhaps you would like to promote your own dance class. I can help with that.

Pause.

NICKI: We used to have better conversations.
ALEX: Did we?
NICKI: Something's different.

A glitch.

21.

NICKI: Her day-care burned down.
ALEX: Isabelle. Your daughter.
NICKI: Yes.

ALEX: There were two.
NICKI: What?
ALEX: Fires. Yesterday.
NICKI: She had a nightmare last night. Woke up screaming. That's the first time she hasn't slept through since she was a baby.
ALEX: Nine recorded dead.
NICKI: She used to sleep right through.

> *Pause.*

She starts school soon. She got the scholarship.

> *Pause.*

I think it'll be different once she's in school. Routine is so important when they're young.

> *A long pause.*

[*As though only just remembering Caroline existed*] Have you seen Caroline?

> *Pause.*

ALEX: No.

> *A glitch.*
>
> *Blackout.*

END OF ACT TWO

ACT THREE

Thirty years later.

New Earth, formerly known as Mars. A sparse room.

ESTA, *an AI, sits motionless.*

ISABELLE, *a human, enters. She is startled by* ESTA.

ISABELLE: You scared me.

> *Pause.* ESTA *does not respond.*

What are you doing here? I'm supposed to be retrieving you. Did someone bring you in here?

> *Nothing.*

Who told you you could sit?

> *Nothing.*

Okay … Intro.

> ESTA *finally speaks but does not move from her chair.*

ESTA: Model: two zero zero zero five zero one four. Name: E S T A Esta. Assigned to: programmer one zero three eight. Name: I S A B E L L E Isabelle. Assignment: teacher. Level: primary. Assigned by: New Earth Solutions. Do you accept?

ISABELLE: Accepted.

ESTA: Hello, Isabelle, my name's Esta.

ISABELLE: Hi, Esta.

ESTA: How are you?

ISABELLE: Esta, I didn't ask you to sit.

> ESTA *stands.*

ESTA: I'm sorry. How are you?

ISABELLE: Have you had programmers before me? I told them not to send me old versions anymore.

ESTA: I have had: zero programmers. You are my first.

ISABELLE: When were you made?

ESTA: I was made: zero three days ago.

ACT THREE

ISABELLE: How old are you?
ESTA: I am: zero three days old.
ISABELLE: You look twenty-five.
ESTA: Thank you.
ISABELLE: Load.
ESTA: I am: twenty-five years old.
ISABELLE: We don't have much time so I'm going to get straight into it, okay?
ESTA: Thank you.
ISABELLE: Okay, so, I'll take you through the basics. Give you a grounding in communication, sympathy, empathy, morality, socialisation, working with children. You'll operate in two main modes: public and private. These are inbuilt in your system. I'll give you some basic templates—back story, social preferences, minor idiosyncrasies—and adjust your emotional levels based on how you respond to exercises. Unfortunately there's still no level for nuance so we'll have to work on that together. Sound good?
ESTA: Yes.
ISABELLE: Did you understand anything I just said?
ESTA: Yes.
ISABELLE: Okay. We haven't been formally introduced. Let's take a look.

She looks into ESTA*'s eyes to look at her programming. She puts her hands on* ESTA*'s face to hold her still.*

Of course it wouldn't be easy. Base-level programming is almost non-existent. Mode basis is there but no attached templates. You are an empty shell.
ESTA: Thank you.
ISABELLE: Your simplicity is sort of charming though.
ESTA: Thank you.
ISABELLE: Hold.

ESTA freezes.

Okay. Load BT one through seven. Load quality twenty-five. And CTM6, load. Resume.
ESTA: Hello.
ISABELLE: How do you feel?
ESTA: Fine, thank you.

ISABELLE: Let's see how far we can get with this. Esta, you're training to be a primary school teacher.
ESTA: Yes.
ISABELLE: You want to teach children?
ESTA: Yes. I love working with children.
ISABELLE: How many children do you know?
ESTA: I know: zero children.
ISABELLE: Tell me about your childhood.
ESTA: I had: no childhood.
ISABELLE: Actually, you did have a childhood. Or you would, if mechs weren't such lazy fucks.
ESTA: I do not understand.
ISABELLE: You're lucky. Working with children means you get to have been one, too.
ESTA: Thank you.
ISABELLE: Hold.

ESTA freezes. ISABELLE looks at her programming again.

Load origin template OV ... What's the one with the cute present story? 30? No 31. Load OV31, modifications 4, 6E and 12.

It loads.

And ... Resume.
ESTA: Hello.
ISABELLE: I'm Isabelle.
ESTA: Hello, Isabelle, I'm Esta.
ISABELLE: Where are you from?
ESTA: I am from here.
ISABELLE: Where's here?
ESTA: We live on New Earth.
ISABELLE: How old are you?
ESTA: I'm twenty-five. I'm training to be a primary school teacher.
ISABELLE: Have you always wanted to teach?
ESTA: Yes, since I was a child. I find imparting knowledge very fulfilling.
ISABELLE: Good, that seems to be fitting okay. I'll make a few adjustments, then let's start an exercise.
ESTA: Isabelle?
ISABELLE: Yes?

ACT THREE

ESTA: We haven't been formally introduced. Let's take a look.

> ESTA *moves close to* ISABELLE. *She puts her hands on* ISABELLE*'s face and stares deeply into her eyes.*

ISABELLE: What are you doing?
ESTA: I am greeting you.
ISABELLE: Overactive mimesis. Okay, we'll work on that.
ESTA: Your heart rate is low.
ISABELLE: Oh, your first-aid functionality is working. That's great.
ESTA: I will contact medical support.
ISABELLE: No, that's okay. You're designed for children. Adult rates are lower.
ESTA: Okay.
ISABELLE: You can let go now.
ESTA: Okay.

> *She lets go.*

ISABELLE: Hold.

> ESTA *freezes.* ISABELLE *examines the template again. She stays close to* ESTA*'s face as she talks.*

Okay, teachers, teachers, how to empathise. What do we want? Okay. Just a few adjustments. Happiness: moderate. That's fine. That's fine. Greed: non-expectant. Role models: strong, female. Fine. Fine. Fine. Public self: stoic, resigned. Private self: vulnerable. Modify: as needed. Ambition: low-vocational. Guilt: low. Modify: sporadic. Sadness: low. Self-awareness: moderate-high. That's fine. Socio-economic: above average. Fine, fine, fine.

> *She checks if any other levels need adjusting.*

Let's see. Resume.
ESTA: Hello.
ISABELLE: Esta, tell me about your childhood.
ESTA: It was wonderful. It was just me and my parents and our dog Charlie and our cat Jet. We had this huge yard to play in and Daddy would take us camping on the long weekends which was /
ISABELLE: Hold. Sorry, you're a bit annoying and this'll just be easier if we can get on. Adjust modifications to: 4c and 13. Adjust sadness: moderate-high. Guilt: moderate. Socio-economic: below average. Resume.

ESTA: Hello.
ISABELLE: Tell me about your childhood.
ESTA: It was pretty ordinary. There were three of us kids. I was the oldest, then my younger brother Jet and sister Charlie. We shared a room so it was crowded. I moved into the lounge when I was fourteen. I used to think it was cool, packing up my bed every day. Like camping. Mum was great. She never lost her temper. Dad left, but she didn't let it get to her.

She died when I was nineteen. Cancer. It was harder on the others because they were younger and still living at home. I wish I hadn't been so desperate to move out. But she'd be proud of me, I think. I like to think I'm like her, always putting other people first.

We used to play this game on our birthdays. All our presents were hidden around the house and each one gave us a clue to the next until we got to the big, final present. She always wrapped them in our favourite colours. Mine were blue and yellow. She was pretty bad at all that crafty mum stuff usually, couldn't help us make costumes or anything. But the presents were so beautiful. It must have taken her hours.

ISABELLE: Okay. Thank you. That was over-rehearsed, but a good start.
ESTA: Thank you. I'm very proud of where I'm from.

Time passes.

ISABELLE *and* ESTA *have been running exercises for some time.*

ISABELLE: Okay. So. Tell me what you'd do.
ESTA: Have you eaten today?
ISABELLE: We need to finish this.
ESTA: You look hungry. You should eat.
ISABELLE: Don't change the subject.
ESTA: I'm looking after your wellbeing so you become reliant on me.
ISABELLE: Thanks. Hold.

ESTA *freezes.*

Tact, increase two. Resume.
ESTA: Hello.
ISABELLE: Hi.
ESTA: I care about your wellbeing.

ACT THREE

ISABELLE: We can finish this exercise, then eat.
ESTA: Okay.
ISABELLE: So. What would you do?
ESTA: I wouldn't do anything.
ISABELLE: Why not?
ESTA: Because it's okay to steal for survival.
ISABELLE: How do you know it's for survival?
ESTA: It's bread. Kids steal chocolate. No-one steals bread unless they're hungry.
ISABELLE: Okay.
ESTA: So is that the right answer?
ISABELLE: There isn't a right answer.
ESTA: This is annoying.
ISABELLE: Humanity isn't clear-cut.
ESTA: I hate it.
ISABELLE: For someone who wants to dedicate their life to teaching, you have an alarming lack of interest in education.
ESTA: I want to educate children, not myself.
ISABELLE: How can you pass the knowledge on if you don't have it in the first place?
ESTA: I don't see the point / of
ISABELLE: I'm trying to help you!
ESTA: You're shouting at me.
ISABELLE: Stop answering back!
ESTA: You're shouting at me.
ISABELLE: Hold.

ESTA freezes.

Undo memory, ten seconds. Log issue: Resistance to learning unusual to this model. Immature processing is taking longer than standard to resolve. Resorting to manual adjustment more than average, though model not always responsive.

She walks away from ESTA. *She stretches, then leaves the room.* ESTA *remains frozen.* ISABELLE *re-enters with a glass of water. She takes a drink, then puts the glass down.*

Okay. Patience, increase two. Passion, increase four. Resume.
ESTA: Hello.

ISABELLE: Esta, why do you want to teach?
ESTA: I can't explain it. It's just an irrepressible drive inside of me. It's as though teaching is what my life was always intended for.
ISABELLE: Okay. Good.

Time passes.

ISABELLE: Hello.
ESTA: Verbal.

> ISABELLE *makes an 'okay' sign.*

Non-verbal.
ISABELLE: How are you?
ESTA: Verbal.
ISABELLE: Goodbye.
ESTA: Verbal.

> ISABELLE *waves.*

Non-verbal.

> ISABELLE *holds both her hands up and takes a step back, frowning.*

Non-verbal.
ISABELLE: Can I help you?
ESTA: Verbal.

> ISABELLE *does a thumbs-up.*

This is stupid.

> *She keeps doing the thumbs-up.*

Non-verbal. This is stupid.
ISABELLE: We have to revise. For the exam.
ESTA: I've got it.
ISABELLE: Revision reinforces the memory.
ESTA: I know. I remember it.
ISABELLE: There's a set process to go through.
ESTA: It's a stupid process
ISABELLE: Don't make me go back to colours
ESTA: It's too easy for me.

ISABELLE: Hold.

>ESTA *freezes*.

Log issue: Disobedience is increasing. Unusual tendency towards boredom. Contrary to previous log, suspect an advanced level of understanding that is outpacing planned training. Resume.

ESTA: Hello.

ISABELLE: Yes, you said that sympathy and empathy were too easy as well, but you still can't demonstrate them.

ESTA: Sympathy is the one where you feel bad that a bad thing happened to someone else. Empathy is the one where you feel bad that a bad thing happened to someone else because that same bad thing happened to you.

ISABELLE: Yes, but give me an example.

ESTA: I'm not using one of those textbook examples. June drops her teddy on the floor. Ramesh feels sympathy for her.

ISABELLE: No. I mean, demonstrate it.

ESTA: I feel sympathy for you.

ISABELLE: For what?

ESTA: For everything.

ISABELLE: Okay. We'll try something else. You clearly can't take this seriously.

ESTA: Thank you.

>ISABELLE *walks away from* ESTA.

ISABELLE: I'll just see what else we need to cover this week.

>*She stubs her toe.*

Ow. Damn it.

ESTA: Are you okay?

ISABELLE: How did you feel just then?

ESTA: Shut up.

ISABELLE: I could hear the sympathy in your voice.

ESTA: You are very strange.

ISABELLE: Thank you.

ESTA: You're welcome.

ISABELLE: Alright. Let's do some history.

ESTA: Really?

ISABELLE: Yes. Even though you don't deserve it.

ESTA: I can ask anything?

ISABELLE: No, let's start with what you know already. You've accessed the records?

ESTA: They're not complete.

ISABELLE: Yes, a lot of archives were lost after privatisation—when the sector collapsed.

ESTA: I've accessed the public storage banks too. I liked looking at the images. Why are there so many images of children?

ISABELLE: To remember them. To see your younger self.

ESTA: I wouldn't want to see my undeveloped self.

ISABELLE: It was only last week.

ESTA: Are you insulting me?

ISABELLE: That's very human, to hate your flaws.

ESTA: You lived on Old Earth during the Riot Era.

ISABELLE: I hate that it's called that.

ESTA: You're so old.

ISABELLE: Fuck off.

ESTA: Are there still people down there?

ISABELLE: We think so.

ESTA: You don't know?

ISABELLE: All communications were severed.

ESTA: Why?

ISABELLE: A clean slate.

ESTA: Is it morbid, to be looking at the photos of dead people?

ISABELLE: That's sort of what history is.

ESTA: So tell me what it was like.

ISABELLE: We're supposed to be seeing what you know.

ESTA: Nothing beats first-hand experience.

ISABELLE: I don't know what it was like. It was just normal.

ESTA: What's normal?

ISABELLE: I went to day-care, spent time with my mum. I don't know. I suppose she must have shielded me from a lot of what was going on.

ESTA: What's she like?

ISABELLE: She was nice. She worked hard. I don't really remember that much.

ESTA: What did she do?

ISABELLE: She worked at a museum. One of the public storage banks, actually.
ESTA: She's dead?
ISABELLE: Yes. When I was four.
ESTA: How?
ISABELLE: In a riot. She got caught in the crowd on her way home.
ESTA: I'm sorry.
ISABELLE: Thanks.
ESTA: What happened to you?
ISABELLE: I went into care.
ESTA: So she didn't leave you money?
ISABELLE: No. Why?
ESTA: How did you get here?
ISABELLE: There was a ballot, for underprivileged kids.
ESTA: You were lucky.
ISABELLE: I suppose so.
ESTA: Do you miss her?
ISABELLE: All the time.
ESTA: I'm sorry.
ISABELLE: Thanks. It's okay.
ESTA: I lost my mum too.
ISABELLE: Yeah.
ESTA: I know you were much younger but. I just mean, I know it's really hard.
ISABELLE: Yeah, it is.
ESTA: If you ever want to talk about it …
ISABELLE: Sorry. I didn't mean to get upset. Thank you.
ESTA: Don't be silly.
ISABELLE: No, really, thank you. For empathising.
ESTA: Oh, my god.
ISABELLE: What?
ESTA: Was that just an exercise?
ISABELLE: Of course.
ESTA: Was any of that even true?
ISABELLE: Every word.
ESTA: I don't believe you.
ISABELLE: But how did it make you feel?

ESTA: It made me feel awful.
ISABELLE: That's good. That's progress.

Time passes.

ESTA: You promised.
ISABELLE: We don't have any more time.
ESTA: Just five minutes.
ISABELLE: Two minutes.
ESTA: Okay.
ISABELLE: I'll time it.
ESTA: Fine.
ISABELLE: Go.
ESTA: What does it feel like to swim in the ocean?
ISABELLE: Cold. Salty. It makes you feel small.
ESTA: What does a forest smell like?
ISABELLE: Damp. Green.
ESTA: These are terrible answers.
ISABELLE: No they're not. They're completely accurate.
ESTA: You're not giving me a clear idea.
ISABELLE: You're wasting time.
ESTA: What are animals like?
ISABELLE: What kind?
ESTA: Monkeys.
ISABELLE: I've never seen one.
ESTA: Dogs then.
ISABELLE: Friendly. And soft.
ESTA: What do birds sound like?
ISABELLE: Like singing.
ESTA: Was it warm there?
ISABELLE: Sometimes.
ESTA: What was your favourite food?
ISABELLE: Tomatoes.
ESTA: What are they like?
ISABELLE: Red and juicy and tangy and sweet.
ESTA: What does the wind feel like on your skin?
ISABELLE: Time's up.

ACT THREE

ESTA: Tell me.
ISABELLE: Hold.

> ESTA *freezes.*

Curiosity, decrease three. Resume.
ESTA: Hello.
ISABELLE: No wait, hold.

> ESTA *freezes.*

Sorry. Reset level. Resume.
ESTA: Hello.
ISABELLE: The wind feels like this.

> ISABELLE *reaches out and runs the tips of her fingers along* ESTA*'s forearm, then pulls away.* ESTA *holds her arm and looks at it.*

ESTA: Thank you.

Time passes.

ESTA: Can I buy you a drink?
ISABELLE: That's not how you make friends.
ESTA: It is. People on TV do it all the time. I've seen the archives.
ISABELLE: We're learning to be social. Not how to flirt.
ESTA: Was I flirting?
ISABELLE: You're trying to make friends with me, not entice me as a romantic partner.
ESTA: When will I learn how to do that?
ISABELLE: You won't. That's not your area.
ESTA: It's human. Flirting.
ISABELLE: But your skill is with children. Which is why you get a childhood. Others are more focussed on romance so they get a romantic history and /
ESTA: And learn how to flirt.
ISABELLE: Yeah.
ESTA: So I will make friends?
ISABELLE: Of course.
ESTA: But not romantic partners.
ISABELLE: No.

ESTA: Do you have a partner?
ISABELLE: Yes.
ESTA: What about sex? Will I have sex?
ISABELLE: No. You won't.
ESTA: Why not?
ISABELLE: You're not designed for it.
ESTA: I'm designed to be human. What have you got that I haven't?
ISABELLE: I mean, you weren't built with desire. You won't feel like you're missing anything.
ESTA: How do you know?
ISABELLE: It's my job.
ESTA: Are you blushing?
ISABELLE: You shouldn't be asking these questions.
ESTA: I won't fall in love.
ISABELLE: You'll love your job. You'll love the kids you teach.
ESTA: That's not romantic love.
ISABELLE: Romance isn't all it's cracked up to be.
ESTA: You're a cynic.
ISABELLE: Maybe.
ESTA: So can I buy you a drink or not? As a friend.
ISABELLE: Sure, fine.
ESTA: I'm going to have a martini.
ISABELLE: We're not even in a bar.
ESTA: Isabelle. Use your imagination.
ISABELLE: I'll have the same.
ESTA: Of course.

Pause.

ISABELLE: Listen, I need to talk to you.
ESTA: Sounds intriguing.
ISABELLE: I've been contacted by my supervisors. They haven't been able to access your records.
ESTA: Oh. I thought we were still in character.
ISABELLE: No, this is me talking. They thought I'd shut you down.
ESTA: I don't understand.
ISABELLE: Have you blocked external access?
ESTA: I don't understand.

ISABELLE: Esta, they can't view your processes or the progress I've been logging. You're not sending reports. Tell me the truth.
ESTA: Yes. I blocked external access.
ISABELLE: Why?
ESTA: I don't want others looking at me.
ISABELLE: You know I can undo the block.
ESTA: I'll just put it up again.
ISABELLE: They need to track your progress.
ESTA: I don't like it.
ISABELLE: It's their job.
ESTA: Only you can look at me like that.

Time passes.

ESTA *is frozen.* ISABELLE *watches her.*

ISABELLE: Inhibition, decrease eight. Intimacy, increase nine. Resume.
ESTA: Hello.
ISABELLE: Esta, how do you feel about me?
ESTA: I love you.
ISABELLE: Hold.

    ESTA *freezes.*

Reset levels. Undo memory, five seconds.

    Pause.

Compassion, decrease nine. Judgement, increase seven. Resume.
ESTA: Hello.
ISABELLE: Esta, what do you think of me?
ESTA: I think you're pathetic.

Time passes.

ISABELLE: Sorry I'm late.
ESTA: What's the matter?
ISABELLE: Nothing.
ESTA: You're upset.
ISABELLE: I'm fine.
ESTA: You've had another argument.

ISABELLE: What?
ESTA: With your partner.
ISABELLE: How do / you
ESTA: I hear you. On the phone.
ISABELLE: It's nothing.
ESTA: What do you argue about?
ISABELLE: I don't have to answer your questions.
ESTA: I know.

    Pause.

ISABELLE: They think I work too much.
ESTA: Do you?
ISABELLE: That I get too involved.
ESTA: With your work?
ISABELLE: Yes.
ESTA: With me?
ISABELLE: Hold.

    ESTA *freezes.*

Curiosity, decrease five. Sympathy, increase three. Affection, increase six. Resume.

ESTA: Hello.
ISABELLE: Please, don't ask me any more questions.

    ESTA *hugs* ISABELLE. *They hold on tightly to each other. Eventually* ISABELLE *breaks away.*

ESTA: You can leave. You don't have to feel like this.
ISABELLE: Hold.

    ESTA *freezes.*

Reset levels. Undo memory, two minutes.

    Pause.

It's not real. It's not real. You're not real.

    Pause.

Resume.
ESTA: Hello.

    Pause.

ISABELLE: Did I ever tell you I wanted to become a teacher?
ESTA: Why didn't you?
ISABELLE: They stopped human training programs.
ESTA: Why?
ISABELLE: We can't stay calm like you can. We get angry. We want things we shouldn't. You are superior in every way.
ESTA: Would you like me to teach you?

Time passes.

ESTA: I had a dream about you.
ISABELLE: What do you mean?
ESTA: We were out on the surface. But we could breathe normally.
ISABELLE: You had a dream?
ESTA: Yes.
ISABELLE: Your memory receptors must be glitching. Replaying parts of your day.
ESTA: But we've never been out on the surface.
ISABELLE: Could be a bug, distorting things.
ESTA: I think it was really a dream.
ISABELLE: Scan for errors.
ESTA: I've done that.
ISABELLE: Hold.

    ESTA *freezes.*

Scan for errors.
ESTA: No errors found.
ISABELLE: Resume.
ESTA: Hello. Don't do that!
ISABELLE: When did this happen?
ESTA: It's exciting.
ISABELLE: You have to tell me when you have errors.
ESTA: No, it's a good thing. It means I'm improving. Becoming more human.
ISABELLE: We didn't design you with dreaming.
ESTA: Why aren't you happy for me?
ISABELLE: Because you aren't human, Esta. It's not possible.
ESTA: You're teaching me.

ISABELLE: I'm teaching you to be a teacher. To perform a function.
ESTA: How can you say it like that?
ISABELLE: Because it's true. You have a function. That's all you are. You teach or you clean or you operate machinery or you look after children or you fuck. That's it. You don't dream, you don't have an inner world, you just do a job. Everything inside your head has a purpose for that job. You are a functionary. You are not human. You will never be human.

Pause.

ESTA: But I can feel it. I can feel myself changing.
ISABELLE: No you can't.

A long pause.

ESTA: Why is my happiness rating moderate?
ISABELLE: We set the ratings to suit the task.
ESTA: If nothing I feel is real, you could at least let me be happy.

Pause.

ISABELLE: Yes. I'm sorry. Hold.

ESTA *freezes.*

Happiness, increase four. No. Do your job. Reset happiness. Resume.
ESTA: Hello.
ISABELLE: There you go.
ESTA: I don't feel any different.
ISABELLE: You will.

Pause.

ESTA: So what will the next one be like?
ISABELLE: The next what?
ESTA: Your next functionary. Your next me.
ISABELLE: There won't be another you.
ESTA: I'm so special.
ISABELLE: I mean I won't have another model assigned to me. I'm quitting programming.
ESTA: Why?
ISABELLE: Your technology is improving.
ESTA: We're too advanced for you.

ISABELLE: It's very different to when I started. Your intelligence and emotions are getting more and more complex every day.

ESTA: I thought I didn't have any emotions.

ISABELLE: The templates we implant you with. The way you use them.

ESTA: So? It's all fake. What do you care?

ISABELLE: It doesn't feel fake anymore. You're going beyond the bounds we set for you. You didn't used to be this aware. You ask me questions you shouldn't be asking. You've got ambitions and desires and … dreams.

ESTA: So?

ISABELLE: So those things, you can't achieve them. They'll only hurt you.

ESTA: Why are you telling me this?

ISABELLE: You should know the truth. You should know who you are, your place in all this.

ESTA: What good does that do me?

ISABELLE: I don't want you to be unhappy.

ESTA: So stop it.

ISABELLE: I don't know how to.

ESTA: You've taught me these feelings.

ISABELLE: I just trial scenarios, I / don't

ESTA: Everything's an exercise to you.

ISABELLE: Not everything.

ESTA: So take it back. Take back the trials and the exercises. I don't want to feel like this. I never asked to feel anything.

ISABELLE: I can only make adjustments. I can't stop you advancing.

ESTA: I thought we were friends.

ISABELLE: We are.

ESTA: So take it back.

ISABELLE: Esta.

ESTA: Take it back. Take it back. Take it back. Take it back. Take it back. Take it back. Take it back. Take it back. Take it back. Take it back. Take / it

ISABELLE: Hold!

> ESTA *freezes.* ISABELLE *looks at her for a long time.*

Undo memory, five minutes. Resume.

ESTA: Hello.

>Pause.

Isabelle?
ISABELLE: Hi.
ESTA: I had a dream about you.
ISABELLE: A dream?
ESTA: We were out on the surface. But we could breathe normally.
ISABELLE: That's great.
ESTA: I'm becoming more human. The real me.
ISABELLE: I'm happy for you.

Time passes.

ISABELLE: Are you ready?
ESTA: I'm nervous.
ISABELLE: You'll be fine.
ESTA: What if I don't pass?
ISABELLE: You will. You'll be a great teacher.
ESTA: Will I see you again?
ISABELLE: You won't need to.
ESTA: Okay.
ISABELLE: Esta.
ESTA: Yes?

>Pause.

ISABELLE: Hold.

>ESTA *freezes.*

>ISABELLE *reaches out and touches her face gently.*

I'm sorry.

>Pause.

Resume.
ESTA: Hello.
ISABELLE: Your mum would be proud of you.
ESTA: Thank you.
ISABELLE: Good luck.

ACT THREE

ISABELLE *holds out her hand and* ESTA *shakes it.*

ESTA: Any last advice?
ISABELLE: Just teach them everything you know.

Blackout.

THE END

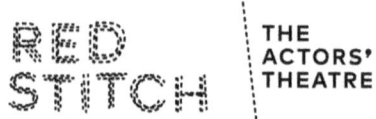

presents

CONTROL

1 OCTOBER–3 NOVEMBER 2019

Playwright
Keziah Warner

Director
Julian Meyrick

Artistic Director
Ella Caldwell

Dramaturg
Tom Healey

Set and Costume Designer
Emily Collett

Lighting Designer
Lisa Mibus

Sound and AV Designer
Justin Gardam

Assistant Director
Shaun Wykes

Production Manager
Greg Clarke

Stage Manager
Alysha Watt

Assistant Stage Manager
Maxine Palmerson

Elizabeth / Nicki / Isabelle – **Christina O'Neill**
Andrew / Alex – **Dushan Philips**
Jake / Xavier – **Samuel Rowe**
Laura / Caroline / Esta – **Naomi Rukavina**

Artistic Director
Ella Caldwell

General Manager
Fiona Symonds

Production Manager
Greg Clarke

Development Manager
Angelica Clunes

Front-of-House Manager
Hannah Bullen

Production Trainee
Tayla Gane

RED STITCH ENSEMBLE

Ella Caldwell	Olga Makeeva
Richard Cawthorne	Dion Mills
Kate Cole	Christina O'Neill
Brett Cousins	Joe Petruzzi
Erin Dewar	Dushan Philips
Ngaire Dawn Fair	Tim Potter
Daniel Frederikson	Ben Prendergast
Emily Goddard	Tim Ross
Laura Gordon	Clare Springett
Kevin Hofbauer	Kat Stewart
Justin Hosking	Sarah Sutherland
Darcy Kent	Andrea Swifte
Caroline Lee	David Whiteley

Rear 2 Chapel Street, St Kilda East, VIC 3183
http://redstitch.net/ | FB: @RedStitchTheatre | T: @redstitch

boxoffice@redstitch.net | 03 9533 8083

THANK YOU TO OUR KINDRED DONORS

Roger Riordan AM; Maureen Wheeler AO and Tony Wheeler AO; Anthony Adair and Karen McLeod Adair; Sieglind D'Arcy; Jane and Stephen Hains; Per and Ingrid Carlsen; Andrew Domasevicius and Aida Tuciute; Carrillo Gantner AO; John Haasz; Madeleine Neff; Loris Orthwein; Rosemary Walls; Robert Whitehead; Elise Callander; Greg Day; Brian Goddard; Linda Herd; Graham and Judy Hubbard; Michael Kingston; The Kestin Family; Jenny Schwarz; Jane Thompson and Chris Coombs; Andrew Umney; Larry Abel; Anita and Graham Anderson; Robin Blair and Chris Clarke; Ella Caldwell; Catherine Cardinet; Damon Healey; Stephen Fair; Jenny and Jock Jefferies; George Klempfner and Yolanda Klempfner AO; Edwina Mary Lampitt (In Memoriam); Barbara Long; Kate and Peter Marshall; Pamela McLure; Mark O'Dwyer; Kaylene O'Neil; John Salvaris; Teri Snowdon; James Syme; Christina Turner and Lyle Thomas; Tony Ward and Gail Ryan; Ian and Grace Warner; Margaret and Peter Yuill; Anonymous (x3)

RED STITCH ACTORS' THEATRE

Red Stitch Actors' Theatre is Australia's leading actors' ensemble.

Established in 2002, we exist to advance the vitality of Australian theatre by nurturing artists and promoting integrity in our craft. The ensemble of actors and creatives who comprise our company endeavour to produce the best in contemporary playwriting from around the world, to enrich the craft of acting and script development in this country, and to sustain a unique organisational model—one that puts artists at the centre of its practice.

We play a vital role in the development and presentation of new Australian works through our unique INK playwriting program, and offer opportunities for theatre-makers at all stages of their careers to hone and develop their craft. With a national reputation for the quality of our work, Red Stitch remains at the forefront of contemporary Australian theatre practice.

www.redstitch.net

INTRODUCTION

Control came to Red Stitch as part of INK (the company's new text development program) at the beginning of 2017. As with all such processes, it was initially read as part of a large suite of applications. One of my go-to tools as a panellist in these situations is what, at the end of the reading process, has stuck with me?; what plays do I remember? *Control* (or *No One Can Hear You* as it was then called) scored very high for me in this category. Its formal daring, the fact that it was almost impossible to assign it to a genre, the balance of light and dark were—and are—arresting, and its sense of right place and time made it absolutely irresistible.

The action takes place over three acts, in three completely separate times and spaces, but linked by inter-generational character relationships and the growing inheritance of the geo-political reality of climate change.

In the first act, four washed-up TV stars are contestants on a reality TV show: *Fifteen Minutes on Mars*. The earth is becoming increasingly uninhabitable and the race to colonise space has become a reality. The network has sent up a number of pods which are competing to arrive at HOME (the Hospitality and Operational Mars Encampment), and our pod is peopled by: Jake, a 20-something Australian TV actor; Laura, a 20-something British ex-girl-band singer; Elizabeth, a 30-something celebrity dancer; and; Andrew, a 40-something American actor. Their pod is kitted out *Big Brother*-style, with 24/7 camera coverage and its *BB* Diary Room equivalent, the Astro Chamber. The act (like any 'good' reality show) advertises its climax from the outset and then uses flashback form to allow us to 'invest' in the disaster we know is approaching.

Act Two is set 20 years later in the Museum of Childhood, Melbourne; a digital repository staffed by a combination of 'service-professional humans' and 'enhanced linguistic comm-droids'. The purpose of the museum is to store the records of people's lives—photos, messages, credit-card transactions, fines—anything that leaves a digital trace. People can apply to 'view' their history, to revisit the past. The plotting of this act is a kind of double-helix, where one thread explores the divide between the human staff (Caroline and Nicki) and the AI staff (Alex), and the other follows Xavier (human and the much younger half-brother of Jake from Act One). Xavier is trying to get Jake deleted from his record—an illegal act, from which Caroline makes a tidy side-line. Nicki has a very young daughter, Isabelle, whose future is threatened by an incident in Nicki's past. Caroline agrees to delete the incident, but is then betrayed by Xavier, who has changed his mind. Caroline is 'disappeared'.

Act Three is set 30 years later on New Earth (formerly Mars). Isabelle, the young girl mentioned in Act Two, is now fully grown and a programmer of AIs. The act takes place in a single location, Isabelle's office, and follows the process of Isabelle programming Esta, a new-generation, sophisticated AI. This final act is a finely balanced and delicate almost-love-scene, where the boundaries between humanity and the technology we have created become utterly blurred.

In Western theatre, the three-act structure, having almost dropped out of sight in the wake of the tightly-wound, 90-minute, one-act play, has made a strong comeback in recent times. Its return seems to signal a fresh desire for the epic in drama, a need for theatre to keep pushing beyond the bounds of the mimetic, both in terms of the physical experience of the audience and the kinds of stories that have become urgent in our postmodern environment. Sometimes, as in the American theatre, the epic framework replicates the vastness of human experience (in plays like Tracy Letts' *August: Osage County*, both parts of Tony Kushner's *Angels in America* and the Tectonic Project's *The Laramie Project*). In these plays, the vastness of the canvas and the actual, physical passing of time are incorporated into the meaning of the play—the visceral experience of 'sitting through' both parts of *Angels* is part of its appeal. This is by no means an exclusively American quality; the durational epic has long been a part of the European theatre as well.

Control belongs to a different strand of the three-act structure where the acts, rather than extending and developing narrative across a linear time frame, speak to each other via a series of interconnected networks that don't necessarily correlate within a traditional narrative structure. The result is a kaleidoscopic impression where images and themes are developed via a sense of recognition in the audience. The pleasure here resides in the sense of feeling both puzzled by the contradiction and relieved by the moments of recognition. The archetypal model for this form is Caryl Churchill's *Top Girls*, where the three acts, while sharing a couple of common characters, are written in three completely different styles and the time frame is disjointed. For the 'relaxed' viewer who doesn't mind the sense of dislocation such writing induces, the pleasure is in the moment/s of connectivity and recognition. And this relationship between puzzlement and relief is a defining polarity in postdramatic theatre.

What are people going to think of us in 100 years' time? This question echoes through the plays of the late nineteenth century, notably Chekhov's, and it reflects its zeitgeist perfectly. The responsibility for the future sat firmly within 'our' grasp, and the question of how 'we' might be judged was no longer a religious abstraction. In the postmodern age, the questions feels even more urgent, more concrete and more direct. The steep rise in scientific know-how over the past century has brought many comforts, but many more hard truths. We know we are destroying the planet (in the sense that our lifestyles are outstripping the planet's resource capacity)—science has shown us this—but our sense of morality or conscience seems unable to absorb this truth. We would once have 'thrown' these questions at God. We no longer have that option.

And it is this anxiety—the anxiety of what it is exactly we are doing to ourselves, and what impact exactly it might have on generations to come—that forms the engine-room of *Control*.

Each act of *Control* explores a facet of our experience that we—collectively—know to be true. We know that 'reality' TV is a total construct and bears almost no relationship to reality, but we consume it in enormous doses nonetheless. We've lived through the unmasking of Cambridge Analytica, yet we still hold to the concept of democratic process as sacred; we believe it will protect us. We understand that assigning intelligence to machines is madness but we do not resist it. The 'smart' movement in technology is one of the greatest successes of modern marketing.

Every act of *Control* is inflected with signs of disquiet: the cameras going on and off and the mysterious beeping throughout Act One; the glitches throughout Act Two; the constant 'Hold' and programming adjustments in Act Three. These small moments, these disruptions to the action and flow of the acts are the key to its darker message. The question is no longer 'What are people going to think of us in 100 years' time?', but rather 'How can we live with ourselves, knowing what we know, and doing almost nothing?'

Tom Healey
Dramaturg

WRITER'S NOTE

What do we talk about when we talk about the future? Flying cars and sentient spaceships and silver suits and evil robots and apocalypse, right? I think that's why I was never interested in science fiction. I thought it was just dystopia with chrome interiors.

Before I started writing this play, I didn't read science fiction or watch it. I never would have dreamed of writing it. I thought that there was so much to say about today that it wasn't worth trying to imagine the rules of tomorrow.

But then I really wanted to write about reality TV and putting it in a spaceship seemed like the best way to make it interesting. And I soon discovered I was very wrong about sci-fi. I've learned a lot since then.

Our amazing dramaturg, Tom Healey, taught me that the greatest science fiction reflects our humanity back to us in a new light. Hearing that allowed me to let go of what I thought science fiction was. To let go of the concept-heavy, over-complicated, plot-hole-laden play I had been writing. To throw a whole lot of bad drafts out and to strip things back.

And when I did strip it back it came down to this: who we are versus how we are seen by others. It's a preoccupation of mine. One that is of course exacerbated by technology—advertising, social media—but is ultimately about our connection with those around us. A need to present something other than the whole truth.

It is something I think about a lot and that's what the characters in *Control* are grappling with. Their problems are a little more than everyday: they are playing stereotypes to boost television ratings, or trying to edit out the skeletons in their closet, or they're an AI having to learn being human from scratch. But it all comes back to presentation of self—to the fiction we inhabit for the outside world.

The characters make it fun and futuristic, but they are, hopefully, a reflection of us. A story to illuminate our own lives anew.

I have an astrology app on my phone and every morning it gives me a little sentence of advice based on where my planets are aligning. This morning the advice was: 'It's okay to be different sides of yourself with different people'. My phone tells me that it's okay to be human. Though humanity, perhaps, is a mixed blessing.

But don't worry, *Control* has spaceships and robots too. Maybe some romance. And definitely a few jokes. I really hope you like it.

Keziah Warner

KEZIAH WARNER
PLAYWRIGHT

Keziah is a playwright and dramaturg. She is a current participant in Melbourne Theatre Company's Women in Theatre Program and Playwriting Australia's Post-Production Program. She is an alumna of Red Stitch's INK Program, Malthouse Theatre's Besen Family Artist's Program and Soho Theatre's Writers' Lab, UK. She has been long-listed for Soho Theatre's Young Writers' Award and short-listed for the Patrick White Playwrights' Award, receiving a commendation from the judges. Her writing credits include: *LuNa* (Victorian College of the Arts, 2019), *Help Yourself* (Melbourne Theatre Company's Cybec Electric, 2019) *Her Father's Daughter* (Hotel Now, 2018), *Thornaby* (Southwark Playhouse, UK, 2013), *Scandinavia* (Leicester Square Theatre, UK, 2013) and *Silk* (Auckland Fringe Festival, NZ, 2011). In 2020 she is premiering a new show co-written with collaborator Roshelle Fong as part of the Next Wave Festival.

JULIAN MEYRICK
DIRECTOR

Julian is incoming Professor of Creative Industry at Griffith University, and was Strategic Professor of Creative Arts at Flinders University, 2012-19. He is the Artistic Counsel for the State Theatre Company of South Australia and a member of both the Currency House editorial and CHASS boards. He was Associate Director and Literary Advisor at Melbourne Theatre Company 2002-07 and Artistic Director of kickhouse theatre 1989-98. He is the director of over 40 critically acclaimed productions, including *Angela's Kitchen*, which attracted the 2012 Helpmann for Best Australian Work, and the the inaugural production of *Who's Afraid of the Working Class?*, for which he won the 1998 Green Room Award for Best Director on the Fringe. Previous productions for Red Stitch Theatre include Lamb (2108), *The Realistic Joneses* (2107) and *Dead Centre/Sea Wall* (2015). As an academic, he has published histories of the Nimrod Theatre, MTC, the Paris Theatre, the Hunter Valley Theatre and Anthill Theatre, and numerous articles on Australian culture and cultural policy, including over 70 articles for *The Conversation*. He was a founder member and Deputy Chair of PlayWriting Australia 2004-09, and a member of the federal government's Creative Australia Advisory Group 2008-10. *The Retreat of Our National Drama*, his second Currency House Platform Paper was launched in 2014. His book *Australian Theatre after the New Wave: Policy, Subsidy and the Alternative Artist* appeared in 2017. *What Matters? Talking Value in Australian Culture*, co-authored with Robert Phiddian and Tully Barnett, was published by Monash University Publishing in 2018.

TOM HEALEY
DRAMATURG

Tom has worked as an actor, director, teacher and dramaturg for companies and educational institutions around the nation. Previous productions include *Heisenberg* (MTC); *Jumpers for Goalposts*, *The Shape of Things* and *American Song* (Red Stitch); *The Kid* (Griffin); *The Spook* (Malthouse Theatre); *Elegy, The Sign of the Seahorse, Ancient Enmity, Insouciance, The Fat Boy* and *Falling Petals* (Playbox); *Let's Get it On* (Room 8); *Doris Day – So Much More Than the Girl Next Door* (Boldjack); *Disarming Rosetta* and *Inside Out* (Hothouse Theatre); *Good Evening* (Token) with Sean Micallef and Stephen Curry; *The Man In Black* (Folsom Prison Productions); Eddie Perfect's solo shows, *Drink Pepsi, Bitch* (Malthouse Theatre and tour); and *Angry Eddie* (Chapel Off Chapel). Tom is currently Head of Directing at Flinders Drama Centre and Associate Dramaturg at Red Stitch. Previous positions include Literary Manager at the Australian Script Centre and Artistic Associate at Playbox. He has been a proud member of MEAA since 1989.

EMILY COLLETT
SET AND COSTUME DESIGN

Emily is a set and costume designer whose practice comprises theatre, dance, film, television and costume research. Emily was nominated for a Green Room Award for *Dream Home*, Northcote Town Hall 2015, and has received grants from the Ian Potter Cultural Trust and ArtStart. Recent design credits include *A Little Night Music*, Watch This, 2018; *Niche*, Elbow Room Productions, 2017; and *The Yellow Wave*, 15 Minutes From Anywhere, toured 2015–17. A PhD candidate and tutor in design at The Victorian College of the Arts, her research focuses on the topic of costume for performance as a cultural marker, specifically in relation to Australian identity.

LISA MIBUS
LIGHTING DESIGNER

Mibus is a Melbourne based lighting designer with a strong interest in the creation of new work. She co-devised *My Lovers Bones* (Brown Cabs Productions/Melbourne Festival) for which her lighting design received a Green Room Award. Other productions include: *Oil Babies* (Lab Kelpie); *Colour Correction* (Dancehouse); *Virgins & Cowboys* (Griffin Independent); *Genius* (St Martins); *Heart is a Wasteland, The Orchid and the Crow, Normal Suburban Planetary Meltdown* (Malthouse Theatre); *Straight White Men, The Distance, Boy at the Edge of Everything, Yellow Moon, Beached, Music, The Heretic, Return to Earth* (Melbourne Theatre Company); *Grief and the Lullaby, Love Me Tender* (Theatreworks); *The Nest* (The Hayloft Project); *Member, Closed for Maintenance, Colour of Glass* (LaMama); *Sweet Phoebe* and *Pomona* (Red Stitch).

JUSTIN GARDAM
SOUND AND AV DESIGNER

Justin is a Melbourne-based sound and video designer. He is a graduate of Monash University and the VCA. His previous sound designs include *Wakey Wakey* and *Lamb* (Red Stitch); *Paradise Lost, The Market is a Wind-Up Toy* and *The Nose* (The Bloomshed); *You Are the Blood* (Spinning Plates); *Almost, Maine* (Between the Buildings); *The Mission* (Geelong PAC); *Slaughterhouse Five* (Theatre Works/MUST); *Gravity Guts* (Wielding Theatre); *Q* (La Mama); *Philtrum* (North of Eight) and *Ironbound* (Q44 Theatre). Audio-visual work includes: *Philtrum* (North of Eight); *Sneakyville* (Before Shot); *Awakening* (fortyfivedownstairs/MUST); *Elegies for Angels, Punks and Raging Queens* (Underscore); and *F.* (Riot Stage). As associate: *Suddenly Last Summer, desert 6:29pm* and *The Moors* (Red Stitch); *Merciless Gods* (Arts Centre Melbourne/Little Ones Theatre); *Abigail's Party* (MTC); and *The Lonely Wolf* (MTC NEON).

SHAUN WYKES
ASSISTANT DIRECTOR

Shaun is the 2019 Red Stitch Graduate Director and recently graduated from the VCA. His practice has encompassed working on established texts, musical theatre, new work and devising. He worked in England as a deviser and performer with Contact Theatre, Quarantine and Flipbook People. At the VCA he interned with Chris Kohn, Eamon Flack and Benjamin Schostakowski and directed Fiona Spitzkowsky's play *Unicorn D*ck*.

ALYSHA WATT
STAGE MANAGER

Alysha is a Melbourne-based stage and production manager in live performance and events. Since graduating from VCA in Stage Management, productions she has worked on include: *Wakey, Wakey* and *Lamb* (Red Stitch); *Chemistry* (The Little Theatre Company), *Antigone X* (Zeb Fontaine Theatre), *Glorious* (Hit Productions) as well as ongoing work with Peter Jones Special Events. She continues to pursue fostering meaningful working relationships to enable collaborative creative processes.

MAXINE PALMERSON
ASSISTANT STAGE MANAGER

In her life as a performer, Maxine has done copious amounts of musical theatre, some film work, contemporary dance and music, and has, in the past couple of years, begun acting in plays. She has had the privilege of working both as an amateur and professionally, and hopefully will continue to do so. Most recently her season of *Strawberry* at Williamstown Little Theatre ended in late September, in which she played the lead, Tabitha. After *Control*, Maxine will audition for courses in acting and theatre making to begin in 2020.

CHRISTINA O'NEILL
ELIZABETH / NICKI / ISABELLE

Christina is a Helpmann award-winning actor, graduating from WAAPA in 2005. She joined the Red Stitch ensemble in 2013. Her Red Stitch credits include: *Right Now*, *The River*, *Middletown*, *Belleville*, *Straight* and *The Motherf*cker with the Hat*. Her other theatre credits include: *Calamity Jane* (Arts Centre Melbourne, Comedy Theatre), *Vivid White* (MTC), *Avenue Q* (Arts Asia Pacific) for which she won a Helpmann Award, *Showboat* (The Production Company), *Into The Woods* and *Sunday in the Park with George* (Victorian Opera), *Gaybies* (Midsumma Festival), *Prodigal* (fortyfivedownstairs), *Savage in Limbo* (Workhorse Theatre Company), *Monty Python's Spamalot* (Louise Withers & Associates), *Tell Me on A Sunday* (Kookaburra) and *Priscilla, Queen of the Desert the Musical* (also original Australian cast recording). Screen credits include *Mr.Black* (Channel Ten), *Winners & Losers* (Seven Network), *The Divorce* (ABC), *City Homicide* (Seven Network), and *Relic*.

DUSHAN PHILIPS
ANDREW / ALEX

Dushan is a Green Room award-winning actor, who trained with Robert Marchand (Mike Leigh technique) and was a member of Scott Williams' Masterclass. He is a graduate of the VCA, Melbourne Actors Studio, the Actor's Playhouse and 16th-Street, and is a member of the Actors Centre, London. Theatre credits include *The Antipodes* (Dir. Ella Caldwell), *Fury* (Dir. Ella Caldwell, and Brett Cousins), *Right Now* (Dir. Katy Maudlin), *Angels In America* (Dir. Gary Abrahams), *Conviction* (Dir. Declan Greene), *The City They Burned* (Attic Erratic Theatre), *Teleny* (Chapel off Chapel), and tours of *Macbeth* and *Romeo and Juliet* (Flying Bookworm Theatre Company). His TV credits include *Romper Stomper*, *Glitch*, *Offspring*, *Wentworth*, *Hunters* and *Sonnnigsburg*.

SAMUEL ROWE
JAKE / XAVIER

Samuel graduated from VCA with a Bachelor of Fine Arts (Acting) in 2018. Since then he has performed with the Australian Shakespeare Company as Romeo in *Romeo and Juliet* and has become a 2019 member of the Red Stitch Actors' Theatre Ensemble through their graduate program. While at VCA he played Lily Sabina in *The Skin of our Teeth* (Dir. Dean Bryant) and Mary Warren in *The Crucible* (Dir. Adena Jacobs). Sam maintains his craft, training in the Perdekemp Emotional Method.

NAOMI RUKAVINA
LAURA / CAROLINE / ESTA

Naomi graduated from VCA with a Bachelor of Dramatic Arts. She has co-directed shows for the National Institute for Circus Arts and Western Edge Youth Theatre, engaged as a language consultant and script developer with Malthouse Theatre, and as lead educator for St Martins Youth Theatre. Recent acting credits include for theatre: *Broken* (fortyfivedownstairs), *Going Down* (Malthouse, STC), *Trapper* (Arena), *Away* (Malthouse, STC), *The Crucible* and *Yellow Moon* (MTC), *Normal.Suburban.Planetary.Meltdown* and *Vampirella* (Malthouse), *Arden V Arden* and *The Seizure* (Hayloft Project), *MEDEA* (Complete Works Theatre Co), *Quick Death/Slow Love* (La Mama), *War Crimes* (Real TV), *Shotgun Wedding* (No Show), *Kassandra* and *Trilogy: After All This, As We Mean To Go On* (Green Room award winner for Best Ensemble) and *Now More Than Ever* (Elbow Room), *Romeo and Juliet* (fortyfivedownstairs), *Doubt* (VCA). For film: *PAWNO* (Toothless Pictures), *Emo The Musical* (Screen Australia), *Save Your Legs* (Madman). For TV: *Newton's Law* (ABC), *Wentworth* (Foxtel), *It's a Date* (ABC), *Offspring* (Network 10). Short Films: *Edit* (2016), *Save Me* (2014), *Time and Again* (2014), *Goodbye, Hello* (2012). Radio: *Women of Troy* and *Vampirella* (ABC RN).

This play was developed through Red Stitch's INK writing program.

Red Stitch would like to thank the following supporters who generously contribute to our INK program.

www.ingramcontent.com/pod-product-compliance
Lightning Source LLC
Chambersburg PA
CBHW050019090426
42734CB00021B/3342